ORAL
HISTORY
CATALOGING
MANUAL

compiled by MARION MATTERS

D1219219

SAA **The Society of American Archivists** *Chicago*

This publication was made possible by a grant from the
National Historical Publications and Records Commission.

Published by:
The Society of American Archivists
600 S. Federal, Suite 504
Chicago, Illinois 60605 U.S.A.
(312) 922-0140
e-mail info@saa.mhs.compuserve.com

Library of Congress Cataloging-in-Publication Data

Matters, Marion E.
    Oral history cataloging manual / compiled by Marion Matters.
       p.   cm.
    Includes bibliographic references and index.
    ISBN 0-931828-97-X
    1. Cataloging of oral history—United States.   I. Title.
Z695.1.H6M38   1995
025.3'482—dc20   95-8672
                                                            CIP

Printed in the United States of America.

© TM   This publication is printed on paper that meets the requirements of the American
        National Standards Institute—Permanence of Paper, ANSI Z39.48-1992.

Contents

Preface and Acknowledgments — vii

Introduction — 1

  Scope of the manual — 2

  Standards and conventions followed — 3

  How the manual is organized — 4

  When to use this manual, *APPM,* or *AACR 2* — 6

  Definitions relating to oral history — 7

  Definitions relating to cataloging — 9

  Note to oral historians — 11

  Note to experienced catalogers — 12

  Note to novice catalogers — 13

CHAPTER 1, General Rules — 14

  1.1 Unit of description — 14

  1.2 Projects, collections, and their component interviews—single description or multiple descriptions — 15

  1.3 Levels of detail in the description — 15

    1.3A Fundamental information — 16

    1.3B Additions to fundamental information — 17

  1.4 Language and script of the description — 18

  1.5 Punctuation — 18

CHAPTER 2, Description of Oral History Interviews, Projects, and Collections — 20

  2.0 GENERAL RULES — 20

    2.0A Scope — 20

    2.0B Sources of information — 20

  2.1 TITLE AREA — 20

    2.1A Individual oral history interviews — 21

    2.1A1 Order of title elements for individual interviews — 21

    2.1A2 Form element in individual interview titles — 21

    2.1A3 Name element in individual interview titles — 21

    2.1A4 Date element in individual interview titles — 22

    2.1B Oral history interviews associated with a project described as a unit — 23

    2.1B1 Order of title elements for projects — 23

    2.1B2 Form element in project titles — 23

Contents

2.1B3 Name element in project titles   23

2.1B4 Date element in project titles   24

2.1C Collections of interviews not associated with a project   24

     2.1C1 Order of elements in collection titles   24

     2.1C2 Form element in collection titles   24

     2.1C3 Name element in collection titles   25

     2.1C4 Date element in collection titles   25

2.1D Repository's entire holdings of oral history materials   25

     2.1D1 Order of elements in repository holdings titles   25

     2.1D2 Form element in repository holdings titles   26

     2.1D3 Name element in repository holdings titles   26

     2.1D4 Date element in repository holdings titles   26

2.1E General material designation   26

2.1F Statement of responsibility   27

2.2 EDITION AREA   27

2.3 MATERIAL (OR TYPE OF PUBLICATION) SPECIFIC DETAILS AREA   28

2.4 DATE AREA   28

2.5 PHYSICAL DESCRIPTION AREA   28

2.5A Preliminary rules   28

     2.5A1 Punctuation   28

     2.5A2 Statement of extent   28

     2.5A3 Single and multiple formats   28

     2.5A4 Original field recordings and copies made for use   29

2.5B Transcripts   29

     2.5B1 Single volume or item (transcripts)   29

     2.5B2 Multiple volumes or items (transcripts)   30

     2.5B3 Dimensions (transcripts)   30

     2.5B4 Electronic form (transcripts)   31

2.5C Sound recordings   32

     2.5C1 Type of sound recording medium and number of physical units (primary statement of extent for sound recordings)   32

     2.5C2 Playing time (sound recordings)   32

     2.5C3 Type of recording (sound recordings)   33

Contents

2.5C4 Playing speed (sound recordings)   33

2.5C5 Number of tracks (sound recordings)   34

2.5C6 Number of sound channels (sound recordings)   34

2.5C7 Dimensions (sound recordings)   34

2.5D Videorecordings   35

2.5D1 Type of recording medium and number of physical units (primary statement of extent for videorecordings)   35

2.5D2 Playing time (videorecordings)   36

2.5D3 Color (videorecordings)   36

2.5D4 Dimensions (videorecordings)   36

2.5E Multiple formats   37

2.5F Supplementary material   37

2.6 SERIES AREA   38

2.7 NOTE AREA   38

2.7A Preliminary rule   38

2.7A1 Punctuation   38

2.7B Notes   38

2.7B1 Biographical information   39

2.7B2 Interview details   40

2.7B3 Scope and content/Abstract   43

2.7B4 Linking entry complexity   46

2.7B5 Additional physical form available   46

2.7B6 Reproduction   47

2.7B7 Location of originals/duplicates   48

2.7B8 Provenance   49

2.7B9 Immediate source of acquisition   49

2.7B10 Restrictions on access   50

2.7B11 Terms governing use and reproduction   50

2.7B12 Cumulative index/finding aids   51

2.7B13 Citation   52

2.7B14 Preferred citation of described materials   52

2.7B15 Publications   53

2.7B16 General note   53

CHAPTER 3, Choice of Access Points   56

3.0 INTRODUCTORY RULES

3.0A Main and added entries   56

3.0B Sources for determining access points 56

3.1 BASIC RULE FOR ENTRY 57

3.1A Oral history interviews with individuals 57

3.1A1 Oral history interview(s) with a single individual—entry under the heading for the name of the individual 57

3.1A2 Oral history interviews with two or more individuals—entry under the heading for name of the predominant participant, or under title 58

3.1B Oral history project interviews—entry under the heading for the project 59

3.1C Collection of oral history interviews not associated with a project—entry under name of individual collector or under title 60

3.1D Repository's entire holdings—entry under the heading for the name of the repository 60

3.1E Collections of uncertain origin—entry under title 61

3.1F Project name change 61

3.2 GENERAL RULES 61

3.2A Alternate entries likely to be sought by catalog users 61

3.2B Form of headings 62

3.2C Added entries must be justified in the description 62

3.3 SPECIFIC RULES 63

3.3A Two or more interviewees 63

3.3B Project interviewees 63

3.3C Interviewers 63

3.3D Corporate bodies associated with an oral history project or collection 64

3.3E Project names 64

3.3F Alternate titles 65

3.3F1 Titles of songs, poems, etc. 65

Examples 67

Tables of USMARC Equivalents for Descriptive Elements 100

Bibliography 104

Index 105

Preface and Acknowledgments

The work of many people went into the production of this manual, which would not have been possible at all without the financial support of the National Historical Publications and Records Commission (NHPRC).

Initial planning, including the grant proposal to NHPRC, was primarily the work of Bruce Bruemmer, Michael Fox, Jim Fogerty, and Lila Goff.

The project contracted with Marion Matters as principal compiler. Matters had assisted Steven Hensen in production of the archival cataloging manual, *Archives, Personal Papers, and Manuscripts* (Society of American Archivists, 1989) and was thus familiar with the process of developing cataloging rules. During compilation of the *Oral History Cataloging Manual*, she consulted frequently with an editorial working group (members listed below). The project's advisory committee (members also listed below) provided valuable expert advice from different professional and organizational perspectives. The advisory committee read drafts very carefully, provided written comments to the compiler and editorial working group, and met once in person. Valerie Brown and Debi Larson, Minnesota Historical Society, provided administrative and clerical support.

In writing the manual, the compiler and editorial working group drew from other cataloging manuals, from catalog records and published guides, from the literature of oral history practice, and from the comments and questions raised by the advisory committee and by other independent reviewers.

Compiling examples. The compiler and editorial committee conducted a thorough sampling of catalog records from RLIN and OCLC, and of entries from selected published guides to oral history collections. The committee also solicited examples from others via electronic *listservs* and notices in newsletters of the Society of American Archivists and Oral History Association.

Literature review. The compiler reviewed the literature of oral history for existing guidelines or recommendations relating to description and cataloging of oral history materials, and for definitions to be used in the manual.

Preliminary drafts. The initial draft was drawn largely from the text of rules in *Archives, Personal Papers, and Manuscripts*. This and other drafts were circulated and discussed among the editorial working group. The group met approximately once a month and also communicated electronically using a *listserv* set up by Bruce Bruemmer. They added examples from the sample records previously identified, wrote new introductory material, and experimented with different presentation formats. Following considerable discussion and more than one intermediate draft, the compiler prepared a draft for circulation to the advisory committee. Their comments were incorporated into the subsequent public draft.

Public draft circulated for comment. The public draft circulated for a three-month comment period. Seventy-five copies were sent out and about fifteen people submitted substantive comments. The Society of American Archivists Committee on Archival Information Exchange also reviewed the manuscript.

Advisory committee meeting and reconciliation of comments. To focus the advisory committee meeting, the compiler assembled a summary and detailed listing of the comments received, both from the advisory committee and from the public reviewers. All substantial issues were resolved at the meeting, but further drafts were required to incorporate the solutions into the manual. Finally, full record examples were added and the compiler prepared an index.

Production. Teresa Brinati, Society of American Archivists, provided editorial support and production management.

PROJECT DIRECTOR	Lila Goff, *Minnesota Historical Society*
PRINCIPAL COMPILER	Marion Matters, *Consultant*
EDITORIAL WORKING GROUP	Bruce Bruemmer, *Charles Babbage Institute, University of Minnesota*
	James Fogerty, *Minnesota Historical Society*
	Michael Fox, *Minnesota Historical Society*
	Lila Goff, *Minnesota Historical Society*
	Stephen Hearn, *University of Minnesota*
ADVISORY COMMITTEE	Arthur Breton, *Archives of American Art*
	Steven Hensen, *Duke University*
	Robert Hiatt, *Cataloging Policy and Support Office, Library of Congress*
	Kim Lady Smith, *Kentucky Historical Society*
	Dale E. Treleven, *Oral History Program, University of California, Los Angeles*
	Martha M. Yee, *UCLA Film and Television Archive*

Introduction

Oral history interviews have become increasingly important as primary sources of historical information. The oral history interview has developed as a distinct intellectual form, sharing some characteristics of deliberately created works, such as monographs, and some characteristics of unselfconscious accumulations, such as archival records. Oral histories are sometimes both produced and managed by separate oral history program units within larger repositories (usually libraries or archives). Small repositories often acquire oral histories created by individuals, schools, or community projects which don't have the resources to undertake long-term preservation and management of their products.

Repositories sometimes produce and publish guides to their oral history collections, and they may keep information about them in card files or in computer databases, but these sources often are separate from the institution's main catalog. Such isolation can be a liability, because many people believe that if it isn't in the catalog (especially, "in the computer"), it doesn't exist.

This manual has been created to help "mainstream" oral history cataloging. These rules respect the characteristics of oral history as a distinct intellectual form while following the conventions of standard cataloging practice.

Because of the affinities between oral history materials and archival records, this manual is based heavily on the archival approach to cataloging. Archival cataloging is characterized by its focus on the context in which materials were created (their provenance) as much as on their content or physical characteristics. It is also characterized by collective description; that is, the description of groups of materials related by provenance. Archival (and oral history) descriptions are created by supplying information extracted from various sources, rather than transcribing information from a chief source of information such as a title page, label, or screen.

This manual assumes general knowledge of cataloging practice, but because it is likely to be consulted both by oral historians and novice catalogers, it includes usage notes that may help to explain unfamiliar terms, concepts, and conventions.

Scope of the manual

These rules are intended for use by archival repositories, libraries, or any institutions that wish to catalog oral history materials. The term *repository* will be used throughout to mean any institution holding oral history materials.

The rules cover:
- *Oral history interviews* described individually, as well as entire *oral history projects* and *oral history collections* described collectively
- Supplying *titles* to identify interviews and projects
- Providing *physical descriptions* of the kinds of materials most commonly associated with oral history interviews (e.g., sound recordings, videorecordings, transcripts)
- Giving *biographical information* about interviewees
- Documenting *interview and project details* (e.g., date, place, name of interviewer, project sponsorship, type of preparation)
- Summarizing the *scope and content* of interviews and projects
- Providing informational *notes* concerning reproductions, location of originals, provenance and source of acquisition, access and use restrictions, indexes and other finding aids, and citations to separate works based on the interviews
- Adding personal name headings, corporate name headings, and title headings as *access points*

The rules do not cover:
- Description of management actions, although the results of such actions (e.g., appraisal, processing, preservation, reference) may be reflected in the bibliographic descriptions created according to the rules. Information about management actions is presumed to be subject to the requirements of individual repositories.
- Subject analysis and indexing, that is, the assignment of specific controlled vocabulary terms or headings to be used as topical access points. It is assumed that repositories using standard lists of headings, such as Library of Congress Subject Headings, will continue to do so.

Standards and conventions followed

The rules that follow are compatible with accepted standards for library and archival cataloging as represented in:

- *Archives, Personal Papers, and Manuscripts: A Cataloging Manual for Archival Repositories, Historical Societies, and Manuscript Libraries*, 2nd ed., 1990 (acronym: *APPM*)
  The standard manual for archival cataloging, covering materials in any physical form that are managed as archives. *APPM* focuses on collective description—of record groups, collections, and series—where the description is created by supplying information extracted from various sources. The note area of description in this manual is based heavily on *APPM*; where appropriate, a reference to the corresponding rule in *APPM* is given.

- *Anglo-American Cataloguing Rules*, 2nd ed., 1988 rev. (acronym: *AACR 2*)
  The standard manual for general library cataloging, covering books, cartographic materials, manuscripts, music, sound recordings, motion pictures and video recordings, graphic materials, computer files, three-dimensional artifacts and realia, serials, and microforms. *AACR 2* focuses on description of individual items, created primarily by transcribing information found on the item's title page, container label, or title screen. The physical description area in this manual is based heavily on *AACR 2*; where appropriate, a reference to the corresponding rule in *AACR 2* is given.

- *USMARC Format for Bibliographic Data*
  The standard format in which catalog records are shared between computer systems in the United States. The USMARC format consists primarily of definitions and three-character *tags* for fields and subfields of bibliographic data. Catalog records that are created according to the rules in *APPM* or *AACR 2* can be tagged with USMARC format tags so that computers can manipulate them. The USMARC format covers any kinds of materials that can be cataloged. (See Examples, p. 67 for examples of USMARC tagging.)

How the manual is organized

Chapter 1 contains certain general rules that apply to all descriptions (e.g., the definition of fundamental information, punctuation).

Like the manual from which it is primarily derived, *APPM*, the rules in Chapter 2 of this manual are organized into the following *areas of description*, whose numbering corresponds to *APPM* and *AACR 2*.

Area of description	Corresponding rule numbers		
	Oral History Cataloging Manual	*APPM*	*AACR 2*
1 Title area	2.1x	1.1x	1.1x 2.1x ... 12.1x
2 Edition area		1.2x	1.2x 2.2x ... 12.2x
3 Material (or type of publication) specific details area			3.3x 5.3x 9.3x 11.3x 12.3x
4 Publication, distribution, etc. area			1.4x 2.4x ... 12.4x
5 Physical description area	2.5x	1.5x	1.5x 2.5x ... 12.5x
6 Series area			1.6x 2.6x ... 12.6x
7 Note area	2.7x	1.7X	1.7x 2.7x ... 12.7x

The shaded sections for areas 3, 4, and 6 apply to the cataloging of other types of material according to *AACR 2*. They are *undefined* (not used) for oral history cataloging and for archival cataloging according to *APPM*. Area 2, Edition, is defined in *APPM* but seldom used in archival cataloging; it is undefined and not used for oral history cataloging.

ACCESS POINTS

The establishment of standardized access points (main and added entries) is considered a separate process in the context of cataloging, so rules for access points are given in their own chapter (3).

IDENTIFICATION OF FUNDAMENTAL INFORMATION

The manual distinguishes between fundamental information—absolutely required to identify the material described and to distinguish it from other material—and other information that enhances a user's ability to evaluate the potential relevance of the material described. Fundamental information for interviews, projects, and collections is specified in tables under rule 1.3A and marked with a ✓ in the right margin next to each applicable rule that follows.

USAGE NOTES

Since many rules are permissive, rather than restrictive, usage notes explain how catalogers and repositories may exercise judgment in applying the rules or in giving additional information.

When to use this manual, APPM, or AACR 2

There are three cataloging options for describing oral history materials. This manual is most appropriate for original oral histories. *Anglo-American Cataloguing Rules* is most appropriate for published material. *Archives, Personal Papers and Manuscripts* is most appropriate for oral histories that are part of a larger archival collection. The following table details these options.

Physical format	Unit of description	Rules to use
Transcript(s) only *or* Sound recording(s) only *or* Videorecording(s) only *or* Multiple physical formats	Single interview with single interviewee *or* Multiple interviews with single interviewee (interviews conducted by same person or program) *or* Multiple interviews, multiple interviewees (project or collection)	*Oral History Cataloging Manual*
Except, optionally: If the material is published, that is, if there is a title page, container label, or title screen for the unit of description that gives *formal title and publication details* (e.g., name of publisher, place of publication, publication date, series designation)		*AACR 2:* Chapter 2 (for transcripts only) Chapter 6 (for sound recordings only) Chapter 7 (for videorecordings only) *or* *AACR 2*, chapter for primary format (2, 6, or 7); treat additional formats as accompanying materials.
Except: If the oral history materials are part of a larger archival unit (e.g., record group, series, collection)		*APPM:* Treat entire body of material as an archival unit of description; *and, optionally,* also make a separate record (or records) for the oral history materials using *Oral History Cataloging Manual.*

Definitions relating to oral history

ORAL HISTORY

The process of deliberately eliciting and preserving, usually in audio or audio and visual recording media, a person's spoken recollections of events and experiences based on first-hand knowledge.

ORAL HISTORY INTERVIEW

A recorded interview, or interviews
- in question-and-answer format (interactive and iterative)
- conducted by an interviewer who has some knowledge of the subject to be discussed
- with a knowledgeable interviewee (often referred to as *narrator*)
- on subjects of historical interest
- intended to be made accessible to a broad spectrum of researchers

ORAL HISTORY PROJECT

Series of oral history interviews focused on documenting a topic, theme, era, place, organization, event, or group of people, conducted according to a plan, usually under the auspices of an institution or a group of cooperating institutions.

ORAL HISTORY PROGRAM

Continuing series of oral history projects under one management.

ORAL HISTORY MATERIALS

The recordings generated during oral history interviews and associated documents intended for use with, or in place of, the recordings.

ORAL HISTORY COLLECTION

Oral history materials from various interviews not associated with an oral history project, usually assembled at some time after their creation by an individual collector, or by a repository for convenience in management or description. A collection, like an oral history project, often has an identifiable theme or focus.

DOCUMENTARY MATERIALS WITH AN ORAL OR SOUND COMPONENT THAT ARE *NOT* CONSIDERED ORAL HISTORY

Recordings of broadcasts (including broadcast journalistic interviews), meetings, conferences, concerts, speeches, autobiographical memoirs, recorded field notes, actuality sounds (e.g., surf, bird songs)—each has an oral or sound component, but none has all the primary characteristics of oral history as an intellectual form defined above. These materials certainly may be important historical sources worthy to be cataloged, but this manual does not address their unique characteristics as intellectual forms. Nothing would preclude using this manual—as far as it applies—to catalog such materials. The cataloger should simply be aware that such materials might have some characteristics that this manual does not address.

ORIGINALS, COPIES, DUPLICATES

The terms *originals*, *copies*, and *duplicates* may be used in different situations, making it difficult to apply a single definition. They will be defined where used.

Definitions relating to catalogs and cataloging

CATALOG

A list of materials contained in a repository or a group of repositories, arranged so that people can use it to find materials when they need them.

A catalog has two primary functions:
- To enable a user to find a particular item. This is called the *finding* function of the catalog.
- To enable a user to find materials that share a common characteristic, such as subject or physical format. This is called the *collocation* (i.e., bringing together) function of the catalog.

A catalog may exist in any of several forms, such as a card file, a book-like list, or a computer database.

Since this manual does not contain instructions for constructing or maintaining a catalog in any of these forms, the novice cataloger may need to consult additional sources, such as those listed in the Bibliography (page 103).

CATALOGING

The process of creating a standard description of an item or group of items to enter (i.e., file) in a catalog. This process involves decisions concerning the content and structure of the description, as well as the way it is filed in the catalog (i.e., determining the access points).

Preparing and filing or entering catalog descriptions for oral history materials not only provides access to local users, but also is the first step toward incorporating them into larger information networks, in which distant users can discover them. Thousands of such catalog records already appear in the international research databases of OCLC and the Research Libraries Group (RLIN).

The best way to integrate oral history materials into existing catalogs and research networks is to begin by following national and international rules and guidelines for cataloging.

CATALOG RECORD

The standard description of an item or group of items entered in a catalog. The standard description is usually also accompanied by standard access points.

ACCESS POINT

A name, term, code, etc., under which a catalog record may be searched and identified, often used interchangeably with *heading* (a name, word, or phrase placed at the head of a catalog entry to provide an access point).

Chapter 3 contains rules for determining some of the access points—personal and corporate name headings and title headings—under which a catalog record might be entered. Guidelines for determining topical, chronological, form/genre, and geographical access points are not given in this manual.

Note to oral historians

The content of this manual reflects guidelines developed by oral historians and rules developed by catalogers. Both are required to assure that information about oral history materials is accessible to its users in catalogs and research networks.

Although this manual assumes a general knowledge of catalogs and cataloging practice, oral historians don't necessarily have to become catalogers to use this manual. They might use it to facilitate communication with catalogers who are used to working with other types of materials. The manual is organized like other cataloging manuals and uses the same terminology. In that context, it gives catalogers information about the characteristics of oral history materials, thereby providing common ground for discussion.

Knowing what kinds of information catalogers need, oral historians can make sure that interview and project documentation provides that information in some form. Catalogers can then apply *their* expertise to transform such "raw data" into standard catalog records.

The tables on pages 16–17 summarize the *fundamental information* that is required for useful catalog records for oral history materials. In the area of physical description (shown in the tables as "statement of quantity or extent"), there are more specific fundamental requirements for different types of material (e.g., sound recordings, videorecordings, transcripts). All fundamental information requirements are marked with a ✓ in the right margin. By providing the cataloger with this information, the oral historian will help ensure an adequate catalog record.

In addition to the fundamental information required for catalog records, other kinds of information are required to support management of an oral history program, as indicated in the *Oral History Evaluation Guidelines* adopted by the Oral History Association. Some of this additional information may be included in catalog records at the discretion of the repository, or it may be handled in separate record-keeping systems.

Note to experienced catalogers

The oral history interview, as a distinct intellectual form, shares some characteristics of deliberately created works, such as monographs, and some characteristics of unself-conscious accumulations, such as archival records.

Physical description rules for oral history cataloging are derived primarily from *Anglo-American Cataloguing Rules*, 2nd. ed., 1988 revision (*AACR 2*), especially chapters 6 and 7; other rules are derived primarily from *Archives, Personal Papers, and Manuscripts: A Cataloging Manual for Archival Repositories, Historical Societies, and Manuscript Libraries*, 2nd. ed., 1989 (*APPM*). One of these manuals is also required for constructing name headings (personal, corporate, geographic).[1]

There are certain notable features of oral history cataloging that may seem unusual or unfamiliar:
- The unit of description is often collective (see Unit of description, rule 1.1, page 14).
  Collective description will be familiar to catalogers used to working with archival materials and *APPM*, but possibly unfamiliar to catalogers used to working with *AACR 2*.
- There is no chief source of information or prescribed sources of information; *all* information in the catalog record is supplied by the cataloger from a variety of sources.
  This, too, will seem normal to *APPM* catalogers and unusual to *AACR 2* catalogers.
- The order of elements in the supplied title is prescribed.

This manual assumes a general knowledge of cataloging practice, but because it may be used also by inexperienced catalogers or by oral historians, it includes many usage notes that an experienced cataloger might find unnecessary.

---

[1] The rules for name headings in *APPM* (chapters 3–6) consist chiefly of verbatim selections from the equivalent chapters of *AACR 2* (chapters 22–25) combined with selected Library of Congress rule interpretations.

Note to novice catalogers

Good cataloging requires broad general knowledge about how information is organized, as well as knowledge of how catalogs are constructed and maintained, and how users may search for information.

In cataloging there are many rules and conventions to follow, not for their own sake, but because the standardized information in well-constructed catalog records is usually easier to manage and to search. This is just as true for small card catalogs and computer databases as it is for research networks that have millions of catalog records.

This manual assumes general knowledge of cataloging practice. While this manual contains many usage notes to explain how the rules should work, it cannot possibly teach cataloging. Chapter 3, Choice of Access Points, probably would present the most problems for the novice. The concepts of *access point* and *entry* may be unfamiliar, and the process of establishing standard access points requires using one of two other manuals: *Archives, Personal Papers and Manuscripts: A Cataloging Manual for Archival Repositories, Historical Societies, and Manuscript Libraries*; or *Anglo-American Cataloguing Rules*, 2nd ed., 1988 revision.

Sources for assistance with cataloging problems might include:
- Advice or tutorials from experienced catalogers
- Workshops conducted by or for professional associations
- Courses in cataloging and information management from a graduate library school
- Internet special-interest mailing lists (often referred to as *listservs)*, such as the LCSHAMC list, covering Library of Congress Subject Headings and USMARC for Archival and Manuscripts Control

The bibliography in this manual (p. 103) contains an annotated list of tools used in cataloging.

CHAPTER 1

GENERAL RULES

1.1 Unit of description

Rule: **In oral history cataloging, the unit of description comprises *all* the oral history materials associated with one of the following:**
- ***an individual oral history interview* (or sequence of interviews with the same person)**
- ***an oral history project***
  Series of oral history interviews focused on documenting a topic, theme, era, place, organization, event, or group of people, conducted according to a plan, usually under the auspices of an institution or a group of cooperating institutions.
- ***a collection of oral history interviews***
  Various interviews not associated with an oral history project, usually assembled at some time after their creation by an individual collector, or by a repository for convenience in management or description. A collection, like an oral history project, may have an identifiable theme or focus.

Rule: ***Oral history materials* consist of the recordings generated during oral history interviews and associated documents intended for use in place of the recordings (e.g., transcripts). Recordings and associated documents in electronic forms will also be considered *materials* for the purpose of description. Give information about all oral history materials associated with an interview—that are held by the repository—in a single description. Do not make separate descriptions for the recording and for the transcript of a single interview if both are held by the repository.**

Give information about all oral history materials associated with an oral history *project* in a single description.

Give information about all oral history materials associated with a *collection* in a single description.

Usage note: In most cases, the unit of description for oral histories is linked to provenance—to the *activities* that generated the materials described—rather than to specific physical items.

An oral history *collection*, as defined above, may reflect an organizing principle other than provenance, but can be similarly treated as a unit of description.

1.2 Projects, collections, and their component interviews—single description or multiple descriptions

Rule: **For each oral history project or collection, create a description for the project or collection as a whole.**

Rule: *Optionally,* **also create a separate description for any or for each individual interview in the project or collection.**

Usage note: Creating a collective description for every *project* makes it possible to give particulars about the project in one place, instead of repeating the same information in descriptions of component interviews. Such a description provides the necessary context for understanding the provenance of individual interviews, whether or not they are described separately.

Collective description may be all that is necessary or possible for some projects and collections. The repository may, however, want to create a separate description for any individual interview within a project or collection. Especially important interviews (as determined by the repository) may warrant individual description.

The *optional* part of this rule means that it is acceptable to provide individual description for all, some, or none of the component interviews in a project or collection.

1.3 Levels of detail in the description
    AACR 2 1.0D
    APPM 1.0D

Rule: **Include in every description enough information**
    • **to identify the material described**
    • **to distinguish it from other material**

Rule: *Optionally,* **give additional information to**
    • **help users evaluate the potential usefulness of the material (this may include additional information about provenance, informational content, physical characteristics, location of copies, and use restrictions)**
    • **guide users to related materials**

Usage note: This manual has rules for more kinds of information than would be given in a typical catalog description of oral history materials. Many are optional but are provided in case they are needed for specific cases. A cataloger should concentrate first on giving the *fundamental information* identified in the following rules.

1.3A   Fundamental information

AACR 2   1.0D1
APPM   1.0D1

Rule: For every description of oral history material, include at least
the following fundamental elements of information.

If an element of fundamental information cannot be determined from any available source, acknowledge the missing
information by making a note of it in the description (see examples under General note, rule 2.7B16, page 53).

Individual oral history interviews

Fundamental elements of information	Rule that applies
Indication of form (i.e., *oral history interview*)	All given as part of Title area, 2.1
Name of interviewee	
Date or inclusive dates of interview(s)	
Statement of quantity or extent, including charac-terization of physical format(s)	Physical description area, 2.5
Name(s) of the interviewer(s)	Both given in Interview details, rule 2.7B2
Language of the interview(s), if other than English	
Summary of the content, nature, and scope of the interview	Scope and content note, 2.7B3
Statement of restrictions on access or use, if any	Restrictions notes, 2.7B10, 2.7B11
Name of the project or collection of which the in-terview is a part, if applicable	Linking entry complex-ity note, 2.7B4

Oral history projects

Fundamental elements of information	Rule that applies
Indication of form (i.e., *oral history interviews*)	All given as part of Title area, 2.1
Name of the project	
Inclusive dates of interviews	
Statement of quantity or extent, including charac-terization of physical format(s)	Physical description area, 2.5
Language(s) of the interviews, if other than English	Given in Interview de-tails note, 2.7B2
Summary of the content, nature, and scope of the project	Both given in Scope and content note, 2.7B3
Name of the person or organization responsible for the development of the project	
Statement of restrictions on access or use, if any	Restrictions notes, 2.7B10, 2.7B11

Oral history collections not associated with a project

Fundamental elements of information	Rule that applies
Name of the collection	All given as part of Title area, 2.1
Indication of form (i.e., *oral history collection*)	
Inclusive dates of interviews in the collection	
Language(s) of the interviews, if other than English	Given in Interview details note, 2.7B2
Statement of quantity or extent, including characterization of physical format(s)	Physical description area, 2.5
Summary of the content, nature, and scope of the collection	Scope and content note, 2.7B3
Statement of restrictions on access or use, if any	Restrictions notes, 2.7B10, 2.7B11

Usage note: The description should answer the basic questions: who, what, when, where, why.

This rule sets out what has been identified as fundamental information in various manuals and guidelines for the practice of oral history. While statements of quantity or extent (Physical description area), interview details, and scope and content notes are considered fundamental information, the repository may include in them more or less detail at its discretion. See the examples for each rule in Chapter 2.

What if fundamental information is just not available? If it doesn't exist, it can't be put in a description. In such cases, however, acknowledge that the information is missing by stating it in a note as instructed above.

1.3B   Additions to fundamental information
APPM   1.0D2

Rule: **Optionally, include any or all of the other information set out in the following rules that is applicable to the material being cataloged.**

Usage note: Common practice is to include only information that is readily available. Some repositories may choose to seek out additional information that is not readily available. Besides the fundamental information recommended in rule 1.3A, many repositories will want to include additional information to help users evaluate whether the described materials may be useful to them and whether they are easily available for use.

The repository must decide what kinds of information its users most require. (Some guidelines will be given in the specific rules that follow.) The repository must also decide what *applicable* and *readily available* mean in the context of its cataloging program, and whether catalogers should seek information that is not readily available.

1.4   Language and script of the description

AACR 2   1.0E
APPM   1.0E

Rule: **Give information in the language and script preferred by the repository and its users.**

1.5   Punctuation

AACR 2   1.0C
APPM   1.0C

Rule: **If possible, begin a new paragraph for each area of description (e.g., title area, physical description area, notes area) and for each *occurrence* of a note or description area.**

► Strong, Paul I. V., interviewee.
Oral history interview with Paul I.V. Strong, 1990 Feb. 14.
Sound recordings: 4 sound cassettes (ca. 60 min. each)
Transcript: 79 p. ; 28 cm.
(In this brief description, the main entry, title, and physical descriptions of two different kinds of items each begin a new paragraph, or a new line, which is equivalent.)

Otherwise, precede each area, other than the first area, or each occurrence of a note, area, etc., by a period, space, dash, space.

► Strong, Paul I. V., interviewee. — Oral history interview with Paul I.V. Strong, 1990 Feb. 14. — Sound recordings: 4 sound cassettes (ca. 60 min. each). — Transcript: 79 p. ; 28 cm.
(The same brief description, this time given as a single paragraph, with each area of description separated by the prescribed punctuation—period, space, dash, space.)

Rule: **Precede each mark of prescribed punctuation by a space and follow it by a space, except for the comma, period, hyphen, and opening and closing parentheses and square brackets. The comma, period, hyphen, and closing parenthesis and square bracket are not preceded by a space; the hyphen and the opening parenthesis and square bracket are not followed by a space.**

Exception. **Do not precede colons used following introductory wording with a space; similarly, do not precede semicolons used as subelement punctuation with a space.**

► Originals held by:
   (Introductory wording for location of originals note; do not precede this colon with a space.)

► Microfiche copy available for purchase; Columbia University oral history collection, part IV; published by Meckler Publishing, Westport, Conn.
   (Subelements—availability of copy, title, publisher—within this note are separated with semicolons as in ordinary narrative writing; do not precede each of these semicolons with a space.)

For *prescribed punctuation* of elements within each area of description, see the rules for each area.

Usage note: This prescribed punctuation follows general ISBD (International Standard Bibliographic Description) principles. It may be used as a space-saving device and to ease integration of oral history catalog records with records for other materials.

CHAPTER 2

DESCRIPTION OF ORAL HISTORY INTERVIEWS, PROJECTS, AND COLLECTIONS

2.0 GENERAL RULES

2.0A Scope

> The rules in this chapter cover the description of:
> - individual oral history interviews, or a sequence of interviews with the same person
> - oral history projects
> - collections of oral history interviews that the repository has determined would be best described collectively

2.0B Sources of information

AACR 2 1.0A
APPM 1.0B

Rule: Take information for the description from any of the following sources, in any order, as necessary to provide the level of fundamental information recommended in rule 1.3A and any additional information desired by the repository.
- abstract, index, or any other available finding aid
- aural content of interview
- container label
- interview or project documentation (e.g., correspondence, donor agreements or releases, grant requests, interviewer worksheets)
- reference sources
- transcript

Usage note: These rules do not require transcription of information from specific sources. Information in all areas of description is supplied by the cataloger from the sources listed above. There is, therefore, no *chief source of information* nor any *prescribed sources* of information, which most catalogers would expect to find defined here.

2.1 TITLE AREA

APPM 1.1

Rule: For each unit of description, supply a title consisting of a
- form element,
- name element, and
- date element

in the order specified in the following rules.

Usage note: Capitalize only the first word of the title and any proper names in the title. This is the capitalization convention established in *AACR 2* Appendix A (A.4A1).

Following the rules for archival cataloging established in *APPM*, *do not* enclose this information in square brackets, even though it is supplied by the cataloger rather than transcribed from a chief source of information.

2.1A   Individual oral history interviews
APPM   1.1B2–5

Usage note: The rules for individual interviews are intended to cover:
- a single interview with an individual
- a sequence of related interviews with an individual (e.g., done by the same interviewer, or as part of the same project)
- a single interview with more than one individual actively participating

2.1A1   Order of title elements for individual interviews

Rule: **Give the title elements in the following order:**

[form element] [name element], [date element]

► Oral history interview with Severo Ornstein, 1990 Mar. 6

2.1A2   Form element in individual interview titles

Rule: **Give the phrase *Oral history interview(s) with* as the form element in the title.**   ✓ Fundamental information

Usage note: The phrase *oral history interview* is more descriptive of content than other terms that have been used to identify interviews. The terms *memoir* or *reminiscence* might be more accurately used to identify self-generated oral materials (i.e., without an interviewer).

2.1A3   Name element in individual interview titles

Rule: **Give the name of the interviewee(s) as the name element in the**   ✓ Fundamental information
title. Give the name(s) in direct order as used in ordinary narrative.

► Oral history interview with Flora Macdonald Rhind

► Oral history interviews with William M. Huntley

► Oral history interview with Mother Hale and Dr. Lorraine Hale

Rule: **If the name of the interviewee is unknown, give instead a characterization of the interviewee.**

►   Oral history interview with a North Dakota homesteader

Usage note: This should be uncommon, since oral history practice manuals and guidelines all specify the name of the interviewee as essential information.

2.1A4   Date element in individual interview titles
APPM   1.1B5

✓ Fundamental information

Rule: **Give the date(s) of the interview(s) as the last element in the title. Separate the date element from the previous element with a comma, space.**

Give at least the year date(s) for any interview(s). *Optionally,* give specific month and day date(s).

Give inclusive dates if interviews were conducted on more than two different dates.

Give actual or approximate dates as directed in the following table. Enclose uncertain dates in square brackets.

Actual dates	
1976	Year date given
1976–1981	Inclusive year dates given; always give year dates in full (i.e., *not* 1976–81)
1976 July	Year and specific month given (*optional*)
1976 July 15	Specific day date given (*optional*)
1983 Dec. 13–1984 Jan.	Specific range of inclusive dates given (*optional*)
Uncertain dates	
[1983?]	Probable date
[ca. 1974]	Approximate date
[not before 1966] [not after 1974]	Terminal date
[1978 or 1979]	One year or the other
[between 1969 and 1981]	Use only for dates less than 20 years apart
[196–]	Decade certain
[195?]	Decade uncertain

22

> ► Oral history interviews with Eugenie Moore Anderson, 1971
> *(Year date of interview or interviews)*

> ► Oral history interview with Hana Takahashi, 1976 July 15
> *(Specific day date of interview, optional)*

> ► Oral history interview with Kenneth and Greta Yackitoonipah, 1970 November 2
> *(Specific day date of interview, optional)*

> ► Oral history interviews with Clement B. Haupers, 1975, 1977
> *(Interviews conducted in two different years)*

> ► Oral history interviews with A. Frank Ellis, 1973–1975
> *(Inclusive dates for interviews conducted on more than two different dates)*

2.1B   Oral history interviews associated with a project described as a unit
APPM   1.1B2–5

Usage note: A project usually has the word *project* in its name and the name is consistently given as a proper noun (spelled with initial capitals).

If in doubt about whether the materials are associated with a project, treat them as a collection (covered by rules 2.1C1–2.1C4) rather than as a project.

2.1B1   Order of title elements for projects

Rule: **Give the title elements in the following order:**

[form element] [name element], [date element]

> ► Oral history interviews of the Northwest Oral History Project, 1982–1985

2.1B2   Form element in project titles

Rule: **Give the phrase *oral history interviews* as the form element in the title.**

✓ Fundamental information

2.1B3   Name element in project titles

Rule: **Give the name of the project as the name element in the title. Give the name in direct order as used in ordinary narrative.**

✓ Fundamental information

> ► Oral history interviews of the Suffragists Oral History Project, 1959–1974

> ► Oral history interviews of the NASW Oral History Project, 1977–1981

> ► Oral history interviews of the Medical College of Pennsylvania Oral History Project on Women in Medicine, 1977–1978

► Oral history interviews of the Barneveld Tornado Oral History Project, 1984

► Oral history interviews of the Eleanor Roosevelt Oral History Project, 1977–1980

► Oral history interviews of The Last Battleship Oral History Project, 1988

► Oral history interviews of the Textile Workers Union of America Oral History Project, 1977–1985

► Oral history interviews of the American Craftspeople Project, 1984–1988

2.1B4 Date element in project titles

Rule: **Give the date(s) of the interview(s) as instructed in rule 2.1A4.** ✓ Fundamental information

If the project continues, so that there is not yet an ending date, substitute the word *ongoing* in square brackets.

► Oral history interviews of the Women in Journalism Oral History Project, 1987–[ongoing]

2.1C Collections of interviews not associated with a project
AACR 2 1.1B2-5

Usage note: A collection consists of oral history materials assembled, often at some time after their creation, by an individual collector, or by a repository for convenience in management or description. A collection, like an oral history project, may have an identifiable theme or focus.

2.1C1 Order of elements in collection titles

Rule: **Give the title elements in the following order:**

[name element] [form element], [date element]

► Banks and banking oral history collection, 1972–1985

Usage note: The order of elements prescribed for collection titles differs from the order prescribed for individual interviews and projects. Each has been established to incorporate a different kind of name element in a title statement that must be understandable on its own.

2.1C2 Form element in collection titles

Rule: **Give the phrase *oral history collection* as the form element in the title.** ✓ Fundamental information

2.1C3   Name element in collection titles

Rule: **Give as the name element in the title a designation that charac-**   ✓ Fundamental
            terizes the scope, content, or source of the collection.   information

►   J. Roman Andrus oral history collection, 1967 Feb.–April
    (J. Roman Andrus was the source *of the collection. He
    conducted interviews with several pioneer residents of
    small Utah towns; he had painted portraits of the
    interviewees. Alternatively, this could have been given the
    title* Utah pioneers oral history collection, *characterizing the
    scope and content.)*

►   Kentucky history oral history collection, 1977–[ongoing]
    *(Various interviews relating in some way to Kentucky
    history, but not part of a named project.)*

►   Women and women's movement oral history collection,
    1972–1989

►   Virginia Durr oral history collection, 1988
    *(Interviews conducted by Virginia Durr with prominent
    Alabamians involved in the civil rights movement and
    organizations focusing on social change. Alternatively, this
    collection could have been given a title reflecting its topical
    content, such as* Alabama civil rights and social change oral
    history collection; *or both source and topic,* Virginia Durr
    oral history collection relating to the civil rights movement
    and social change in Alabama.*)*

2.1C4   Date element in collection titles

Rule: **Give the date(s) of the interview(s) as instructed in rule 2.1A4**   ✓ Fundamental
            and 2.1B4.   information

2.1D   Repository's entire holdings of oral history materials

Usage note: A catalog record for a repository's entire holdings may be ap-
            propriate in a statewide or regional resource guide, union catalog,
            or research network, especially when cataloging the repository's
            project and individual interview holdings is not possible.

2.1D1   Order of elements in repository holdings titles

Rule: **Give the title elements in the following order:**

            [form element] [name element], [date element]

            ►   Oral history collection of the Manhasset Public Library,
            1953–1988

2.1D2   Form element in repository holdings titles

Rule: Give the phrase *oral history collection* as the form element in   √ Fundamental
                     the title.   information

2.1D3   Name element in repository holdings titles

Rule: Give the name of the repository as the name element in the   √ Fundamental
                     title. Give the name in direct order as used in ordinary narra-   information
                     tive.

Rule: *Optionally,* if the location of the repository is not clear from the
                     name element in the title, and if the location of the repository
                     would help to identify the collection and distinguish it from
                     others, give the location in parentheses following the name of
                     the repository.

                     ► Oral history collection of the Consumers Union of United
                     States Archives, 1972–1979

                     ► Oral history collection of the Friars of the Atonement Ar-
                     chives, 1986–1988

                     ► Oral history collection of the United States Senate Historical
                     Office, 1976–1985

                     ► Oral history collection of the Archives of Cooperative Luther-
                     anism, 1976–1985

                     ► Oral history collection of the Chase Manhattan Corporation
                     Archives, 1960–1987

                     ► Oral history collection of the Research Foundation for Jewish
                     Immigration, [ca. 1971]–1984

                     ► Oral history collection of the Portland Historical Association
                     (Louisville, Ky.), 1976–1977

2.1D4   Date element in repository holdings titles

Rule: Give the date(s) of the interview(s) as instructed in rule 2.1A4   √ Fundamental
                     and 2.1B4.   information

2.1E   General material designation

            AACR 2   1.1C
            APPM   1.1C

Rule: If the unit of description consists solely of a transcript or tran-
                     scripts as ordinary text on paper, or if it consists of material in
                     multiple physical formats, *do not* give a general material desig-
                     nation.

Rule: **Optionally, if the unit being cataloged consists *solely* of materials in one of the physical formats in the list below, give the term from the list following the date element in the title.**

computer file	sound recording
microform	videorecording

Enclose the general material designation in square brackets ([ ]).

► History of Graphic Arts Workshop oral history collection, 1987–1990 [sound recording]

► Oral history interview with Austen D. Warburton, 1989 [videorecording]

► Oral history interviews of the Community Development Oral History Project, 1990–1991 [videorecording]

► Oral history collection of the United States Senate Historical Office, 1976–1985 [microform]

Usage note: The general material designation that may be used in conjunction with titles generally functions as an "early warning" that the material being described requires some special equipment for use.

General material designations come from the list of specified terms published in *AACR 2* (rule 1.1C, list 2). They may not be invented locally.

2.1F   Statement of responsibility

Rule: **Do not supply a statement of responsibility for oral history materials. Instead, give information about responsibility in notes (see Interview details, rule 2.7B2, page 40; or General note, rule 2.7B16, page 53).**

2.2   EDITION AREA

Rule: **Do not supply an edition statement for oral history materials. Instead, give information about versions or "states" of oral history materials in a note.**

Usage note: Transcripts of oral history interviews often are edited before being made public, and information about editorial intervention should be communicated to users of the transcripts. It should *not* be considered an edition statement, however. Give such information in a note, if desired (see General note, rule 2.7B16, page 53).

2.3   MATERIAL (OR TYPE OF PUBLICATION) SPECIFIC DETAILS AREA

Usage note: Do not use this area for oral history materials.

2.4   DATE AREA
           APPM   1.4

Rule: For oral history materials, as for archival materials, include the date(s) as part of the Title area (see rules in 2.1).

2.5   PHYSICAL DESCRIPTION AREA
           AACR 2   1.5
           APPM   1.5

2.5A   Preliminary rules

2.5A1   Punctuation
           AACR 2   1.5A1
           APPM   1.5A1

Rule: If this area is not given as a separate paragraph, precede it by a period, space, dash, space.

Rule: Precede *other physical details* by a space, colon, space.

Rule: Precede the *dimensions* by a space, semicolon, space.

2.5A2   Statement of extent
           APPM   1.5B1–3

Rule: Give the statement of the extent in terms appropriate for the format(s) of the materials being cataloged, as directed in the following rules.

                    If a detailed statement of extent would be potentially confusing, give instead a brief statement of extent in this area of description and explain it further in a note. (See General note, rule 2.7B16, page 53.)

2.5A3   Single and multiple formats

Rule: If the unit of description consists of materials in a single physical format, give the statement of extent as instructed in the rules for the appropriate format.
                    • transcripts (text on paper or in electronic form), rules 2.5B1–2.5B4
                    • sound recordings, rules, 2.5C1–2.5C7
                    • videorecordings, rules 2.5D1–2.5D4

Rule: If the unit of description consists of materials in more than one physical format, give a *separate statement of extent for each format,* **using the rules for the appropriate format (see also rule 2.5E).**

Usage note: These rules provide only for the most common physical formats: sound recordings on tape or cassette, videorecordings on tape or cassette, and transcripts on paper. For other formats (e.g., sound discs, motion picture film), consult the physical description rules in the appropriate chapter of *AACR 2.*

2.5A4   Original field recordings and copies made for use

Rule: **Give the statement(s) of extent in terms of the physical format(s) available for *use,* as directed in the following rules.**

Rule: ***Optionally,* also give statements of extent for original field recordings if they are held by the repository but are not the items actually used.**

Usage note: Seldom is an original field recording of an oral history interview made available for public use. The repository may make copies in a conveniently usable format or may substitute transcripts.

In general, users first need information about the format that they must *use,* rather than about the format of the original field recording, if they are different. In the physical description area, therefore, always give information about the format(s) available for use.

On the other hand, the repository should maintain information about the original field recording(s) and copy generations, and sometimes this information is required by users. The repository should make such information available to users when necessary. A repository *may* give such information in the physical description area using multiple physical descriptions, as instructed in rule 2.5A3, or in a note.

2.5B   Transcripts
AACR 2   1.5B1, 2.5B1
APPM   1.5B1–3

2.5B1   Single volume or item (transcripts)

Rule: **For a transcript (verbatim or edited text of an oral history interview) that is presented as text on paper in a single volume or item, give the number of pages or leaves.**

✓ Fundamental information

▶   115 p.

▶   97 leaves

Usage note: According to *AACR 2* rule 2.5B1, if the leaves in a volume contain text on both sides, each side is a page; count the number of *pages.*

If the leaves contain text on one side only, count the number of *leaves*. Abbreviate *page(s)* as *p.*, but spell out *leaf* or *leaves*.

2.5B2   **Multiple volumes or items (transcripts)**

Rule: **If the transcript occupies more than one volume, filing unit**   √ Fundamental
               (e.g., folder), or container, give the number of volumes, filing   information
               units, or containers. *Optionally,* **also give the total number of**
               pages, leaves, filing units or containers in parentheses.

►   2 v.

►   3 folders

►   15 boxes

►   3 v. (451 leaves)

►   3 folders (336 leaves)

►   6 boxes (72 v.)

Rule: ***Alternatively,*** **give the number of cubic or linear feet.** ***Optional-***
               ly, **give also the number of containers, volumes, filing units,**
               volumes, or items in parentheses.

►   32 linear ft.

►   4 cubic ft. (4 boxes)

Usage note: The abbreviations *p.* for *page* or *pages, v.* for *volume* or *volumes*,
               and *ft.* for *foot* or *feet* are authorized in *AACR 2*, appendix B, along
               with other authorized abbreviations. In this list there is no autho-
               rized abbreviation for *cubic* or *linear,* so each should be spelled
               out.

               Since there are so many acceptable options for the statement of
               extent, the repository should choose one for individual interviews
               and one for projects and collections and be consistent. For exam-
               ple, the use of linear or cubic feet may be appropriate only for
               archival repositories that routinely describe large collections of
               materials. Repositories may want to give the number of pages/
               leaves for single volumes/items, and the number of volumes,
               items, or filing units for multiple volumes/items.

2.5B3   **Dimensions (transcripts)**
           AACR 2   1.5D, 2.5D
           APPM   1.5D

Rule: **Give the height of a transcript in centimeters to the next whole**
               centimeter up.

►   83 p. ; 28 cm.

Add the width if it is less than half the height or greater than the height.

Rule: **Give the height of a bound volume or case in centimeters, to the next whole centimeter.**

▶   1 v. (131 leaves) ; 26 cm.

Add the width if it is either less than half the height or greater than the height.

▶   1 item (70 p. in case) ; 20 x 24 cm.

Usage note: Oral history transcripts are most frequently packaged in 8-1/2-x-11-inch or other standard formats. Catalogers should not worry too much about giving dimensions unless the dimensions are so odd as to affect use or storage.

2.5B4   Electronic form (transcripts)

Rule: **If the text of a transcript is made available in a computer-related medium or in electronic form (e.g., word processing file), give the extent in terms of one of the following:**
> ✓ Fundamental information

  • **the number of units of a physical medium (e.g., computer disk) and its dimensions (e.g., 5-1/4 in.)**
  • **the number of units designated as *computer file(s)* and their size (or range of sizes) in number of bytes**

▶   1 computer disk ; 5-1/4 in.

▶   1 computer file ; 176K

▶   10 computer files ; ca. 100K–600K each

If necessary, give additional details concerning format and availability in a note.

Rule: *Optionally,* **give information about the hard copy in the physical description area and give information about the electronic form in a note as directed in Additional physical form available, rule 2.7B5, page 46.**

Usage note: Rules for describing works in electronic form—especially rules for physical description—are likely to change as electronic storage, communication, and access methods change. The electronic format may come to be considered the primary "use copy." This "rule" should be considered provisional, to give catalogers some guidance during a transitional period.

2.5C   Sound recordings
AACR 2 6.5

Rule: **Give, as a minimum:**
- **type of recording medium (specific material designation)**
- **number of physical units of the medium**

Rule: ***Optionally*, also give, in this order:**
- **playing time**
- **type of recording**
- **playing speed**
- **number of tracks**
- **number of sound channels**
- **dimensions**

2.5C1   Type of sound recording medium and number of physical units (primary statement of extent for sound recordings)
AACR 2 6.5B1

Rule: **Give as the primary statement of extent the number of physical units of a sound recording. Give the number of parts in arabic numerals and one of the following specific material designations as appropriate.**

> sound cassette
> sound tape reel

▶ 1 sound tape reel

▶ 2 sound cassettes

Usage note: These two specific material designations probably will account for all but the rarest circumstances. If neither is appropriate, consult *AACR 2*, rule 6.5B1.

2.5C2   Playing time (sound recordings)
AACR 2 6.5B2

Rule: **Give the playing time in terms of number of minutes or hours as appropriate. Enclose the playing time in parentheses following the primary statement of extent.**

▶ 1 sound cassette (50 min.)

▶ 5 sound tape reels (4 hr., 20 min.)

If the playing time is not known or readily available, give an approximate time in number of minutes or hours as appropriate.

► 1 sound tape reel (ca. 45 min.)

► 10 sound cassettes (ca. 10 hr.)

Optionally, **if the unit being cataloged consists of multiple parts and each part has an approximate uniform playing time, give the playing time of each part followed by** *each.* **Otherwise, give the total duration as specified above.**

► 5 sound cassettes (60 min. each)

2.5C3 Type of recording (sound recordings)
AACR 2 6.5C2

Rule: **Give the type of recording (i.e., the way in which the sound is encoded on the item).**

► 1 sound cassette (60 min.) : analog

Usage note: The two basic choices are *analog* and *digital,* but most oral histories will have been recorded on analog tape reels or cassettes. This may change with the adoption of newer technologies.

Usage note: Type of recording, playing speed, number of tracks, number of sound channels, and recording and reproduction characteristics, constitute *other physical details* for the purposes of prescribed punctuation. Thus, the first element given in this sequence is preceded by a space, colon, space, according to Punctuation, rule 2.5A1, page 28. Elements in the sequence are separated by a comma, space.

2.5C4 Playing speed (sound recordings)
AACR 2 6.5C3

Rule: **Give the playing speed of an analog tape in inches per second (*ips*), following the type of recording. Separate the playing speed from the type of recording by a comma, space.**

► 1 sound tape reel (16 min.) : analog, 7-1/2 ips

► 1 sound cassette (60 min.) : analog, 1-5/16 ips

Rule: **Do not give the playing speed if it is standard for the type of item (e.g., 1-7/8 inches per second for analog tape cassette).**

Usage note: See second usage note under Type of recording (sound recordings), rule 2.5C3, page 33.

2.5C5   Number of tracks (sound recordings)
AACR 2   6.5C6

Rule: **Give the number of tracks, unless the number of tracks is standard for the item (e.g., the standard number of tracks for an analog cassette is 4).**

Usage note: Most oral history use copies will have been recorded on standard media, so there should be nothing to record here. If there is, see also second usage note under Type of recording (sound recordings), rule 2.5C3, page 33.

2.5C6   Number of sound channels (sound recordings)
AACR 2   6.5C7

Rule: **Give the number of sound channels, if the information is readily available, using one of the following terms as appropriate:**

> mono.
> stereo.
> quad.

►   1 sound tape reel (16 min.) : analog, 7-1/2 ips, mono.

►   1 sound cassette (60 min.) : analog, 1-5/16 ips, mono.

Usage note: See usage note under Type of recording (sound recordings), rule 2.5C3, page 33.

2.5C7   Dimensions (sound recordings)
AACR 2   6.5D

Rule: **Give the dimensions of a sound recording as instructed below.**

Usage note: According to the punctuation prescribed in rule 2.5A1, precede dimensions with a semicolon, space.

Rule: <u>Sound cassettes</u>. **Give the dimensions of a cassette if other than the standard dimensions (e.g., the standard dimension of an analog cassette is 3-7/8 x 2-1/2 in.).**

►   1 sound cassette (85 min.) : analog ; 7-1/4 x 3-1/2 in.

Give the width of a tape if other than the standard width (e.g., the standard width of an analog tape is 1/8 in.).

►   1 sound cassette (85 min.) : analog ; 7-1/4 x 3-1/2 in., 1/2 in. tape

34

Rule: <u>**Sound tape reels**</u>. **Give the diameter of a reel in inches.**

►   1 sound tape reel (15 min.) : analog, 15 ips. ; 7 in.

Give the width of a tape in fractions of an inch if other than the standard width (1/4 in.).

►   1 sound tape reel (15 min.) : analog, 15 ips. ; 7 in., 1/2 in. tape.

2.5D   Videorecordings
AACR 2   7.5

√ Fundamental
  information

Rule: Give, as a minimum:
- type of recording medium
- number of physical units of the medium

Rule: *Optionally*, also give:
- playing time
- color
- dimensions

2.5D1   Type of recording medium and number of physical units (primary statement of extent for videorecordings)
AACR 2   7.5B1

√ Fundamental
  information

Rule: Give as the primary statement of extent the number of physical units of videorecording. Give the number of units in arabic numerals and one of the following specific material designations as appropriate:

> videocassette
> videoreel

►   1 videocassette

►   6 videoreels

Rule: Give a trade name or other similar specification (e.g., VHS, U-Matic) for playback system or format if the use of the item is conditional upon this information. Give the information in parentheses following the specific material designation.

►   1 videocassette (VHS)

►   2 videocassettes (Beta)

►   1 videocassette (U-Matic)

Rule: Give the generation of the copy in a note (see examples under General note, rule 2.7B16, page 53).

Usage note: As instructed in rule 2.5A4, give physical description information
                 for the materials that actually will be *used,* if different from origi-
                 nal field recordings.

                 If oral history interviews have been recorded in video format, they
                 will most likely be on cassettes. It is possible that videodiscs might
                 be used for storage and reproduction of oral history materials; con-
                 sult *AACR 2,* Chapter 7, for applicable rules.

2.5D2   Playing time (videorecordings)
           AACR 2   7.5B2

Rule: **Give the playing time in terms of the number of minutes or**   √ Fundamental
                 hours as appropriate. Give the information in its own set of   information
                 parentheses following the specific material designation.

                 ►   1 videocassette (1 hr.)

                 ►   1 videocassette (U-Matic) (66 min.)

                 ►   2 videocassettes (103 min.)

                 If the exact playing time is not readily available, give an
                 approximate time in terms of number of minutes or hours as
                 appropriate.

                 ►   1 videocassette (ca. 1 hr.)

                 ►   2 videocassettes (ca. 2 hr., 15 min.)

                 ►   3 videocassettes (Beta) (ca. 90 min.)

Rule: *Alternatively,* **if the unit being cataloged consists of multiple**
                 parts and each part has an approximate uniform playing time,
                 give the playing time of each part followed by *each.* **Otherwise,**
                 give the total duration as specified above.

                 ►   3 videocassettes (ca. 30 min. each)
                         or

                 ►   3 videocassettes (ca. 90 min.)

2.5D3   Color (videorecordings)
           AACR 2   7.5C4

Rule: **Give the abbreviation** *col.* **or** *b&w* **to indicate whether an item**
                 is in color or black and white.

                 ►   1 videocassette (90 min.) : col.

2.5D4   Dimensions (videorecordings)
           AACR 2   7.5D

Rule: **Give the gauge (width) of a videotape in inches or millimeters.**

                 ►   2 videocassettes (48 min.) : b&w ; 1/2 in.

                 ►   1 videoreel (15 min.) : col. ; 1 in.

2.5E Multiple formats
APPM   1.5B1

√ Fundamental
  information

Rule: **If the unit of description consists of oral history materials in multiple physical formats, give a separate statement of extent for each format.**

► 350 p.
  5 sound cassettes (60 min. each)

Rule: *Optionally,* **precede each separate statement of extent by a form of material designation as an introductory word or phrase. The most common form of material designations would be** *transcript(s), sound recording(s),* **and** *videorecording(s).*

Follow the introductory word or phrase with a colon, space.

► Transcript: 350 p.
  Sound recordings: 5 sound cassettes (60 min. each)

► Videorecordings: 4 videocassettes (1 hr. each)
  Transcripts: 4 v.

► Sound recordings: 901 sound tape reels
  Transcripts: 970 items

Usage note: The colon following an introductory word or phrase should not be preceded by a space; it is not prescribed punctuation governed by rule. Note: the introductory word or phrase is not a substitute for the *specific material designation* covered by rules 2.5C1 and 2.5D1; nor is it equivalent to the *general material designation* covered by rule 2.1E.

2.5F Supplementary material
AACR 2   1.9A, 1.9B

Rule: **Treat small quantities of letters, photographs, or other material assembled to illustrate or support statements made in oral history interviews as** *supplementary materials.* **Do** *not* **give a separate statement of extent for supplementary materials. Instead, give information about supplementary materials in a note (see General note, rule 2.7B16, page 53).**

Rule: *Optionally,* **if the quantity of materials is large enough or significant enough in its own right, as determined by the repository, treat the entire assemblage as an archival collection and make a separate description for it.**

Usage note: If the repository treats the supplementary materials as an archival collection, it should use *APPM* rules for description.

2.6   SERIES AREA

Usage note: The concept of *bibliographic series* does not apply in oral history cataloging according to this manual. If the cataloger finds that the unit of description *is* identified on a title page (or title page substitute, container label, or title screen) as part of a bibliographic series, it probably means that the unit should be described using *AACR 2*—at least for areas of description 1–6.

Usage note: Identify a *project,* of which an interview may form a part, according to Linking entry complexity, rule 2.7B4, page 46.

2.7   NOTE AREA
AACR 2   1.7
APPM   1.7

2.7A   Preliminary rule

2.7A1   Punctuation
AACR 2   1.7A1
APPM   1.7A1

Rule: **If this area is not given as a separate paragraph, precede it by a period, space, dash, space.**

Rule: **Separate introductory wording from the main content of a note by a colon, space.**

Rule: **Separate distinct subelements of a note not governed by normal rules of narrative punctuation by a semicolon, space.**

2.7B   Notes

Rule: **As specified in rule 1.3A, give, as a minimum:**
  * **interview details**
  * **scope and content/abstract**

In addition, give, in any order desired by the repository, any or all of the notes set out in the following rules that are applicable to the material being cataloged.

Give information as separate notes (e.g., in separate sentences, paragraphs, or data fields) or, *optionally,* **combine them when necessary or appropriate.**

Usage note: The examples that follow generally show information as it would be given in separate notes.

2.7B1   Biographical information
APPM   1.7B1

Rule: **Record briefly any significant information on the interview-
              ee(s) required to give appropriate context for the interview.**

Usage note: In various oral history manuals concerning the practice of oral
              history, the following kinds of information have been identified as
              potentially valuable to users of oral history materials.

• other or former names	• family background
• gender	• education, including school(s)
• birth year	attended
• birthplace	• date of marriage
• race	• spouse's occupation
• ethnicity	• number and gender of children
• nationality	• occupation(s) with dates
• dialect (especially for folklore	• political and organizational
uses)	affiliation(s)
• number of siblings	• religion
• parents' names	• place of residence
• parents' occupations	• economic circumstances
• place of upbringing	• decorations and qualifications

Not all of this information is likely to be readily available to the
cataloger. The repository or the individual cataloger must decide
which available information to use and whether to seek additional
information that is not readily available.

The length of the note and amount of detail given are also matters
for local decisions and individual cataloger's judgment. The biographical note given in a catalog record may be a brief summary,
with additional biographical information given in a separate finding aid, as is often done for archival materials.

Some repositories choose to give occupation prominence in the description of an interview, usually by giving this information first,
sometimes by giving it as the only biographical information.

For the benefit of all users, give full place names (e.g., state as
well as county or city) whenever the location cannot reliably be in-
ferred, avoid abbreviations, and explain acronyms. When referring
to an event, do not assume that all users will know when, where, or
why the event occurred; give the information explicitly. When referring to persons and organizations, do not assume that all users
will know who or what they are.

▶   Regent, University of California, 1959–1961, 1962–1977.

▶ Clara ("Mother") Hale and Dr. Lorraine Hale are the founders of Hale House (New York, N.Y.), a temporary home for children of drug addicted parents.

▶ John Meredith played traditional Australian music at bush dances for many years. He began recording bush music in 1953.

▶ Graham Bell Fairchild was born in 1906 in Washington, D.C. He was introduced to tropical biology in his youth when he visited the Barro Colorado Island (BCI) research station of the Canal Zone Biological Area with his father, David Grandison Fairchild. He received a B.S., M.S., and Ph.D. in entomology from Harvard University, where he studied the collections at the Museum of Comparative Zoology (MCZ).

▶ Harry Robbins Haldeman was born in 1926 in Los Angeles and attended schools in the Los Angeles area, culminating in a B.A. in business administration from UCLA in 1948. He spent 20 years (1949–68) with the J. Walter Thompson Co. in New York, San Francisco and Los Angeles; served in the Richard M. Nixon Administration (1969–73) and was president of the Murdock Hotels Corporation in Los Angeles (1979–85). From 1965 to 1967, Haldeman served as an ex officio member of the University of California Board of Regents, when he was president of the Alumni Association of University of California, Los Angeles. In 1968, Governor Ronald W. Reagan, who had earlier named Haldeman to the Coordinating Council for Higher Education, appointed him to a full-term regent's seat. He officially left the board, however, in January of 1969, after becoming Assistant to the President of the United States (White House Chief of Staff) in the Nixon Administration.

2.7B2 Interview details

Individual oral history interviews

Rule: Give, as a minimum, the following information:
- date(s) of interview(s)
- name of interviewer
- language of the interview(s), if other than English

✓ Fundamental information

Rule: *Optionally*, also give the following information:
- place(s) of interview(s)
- names of other persons present
- sponsorship and/or source of funding
- circumstances of interviews, including type of preparation

Usage note: The date(s) will already have been given in the title area (see rule 2.1A4), but should be given again here for clarity and to accommodate detailed date specifications.

40

While the *content* of this note is specified, the repository has considerable freedom to choose the *length, amount of detail,* and *form* or *style* used.

► Interviewed by Gary W. Hull on four occasions from 16 July to 19 August 1977 in Waco, Texas.

► Interviewed in Spanish by Leonardo Estrada twice on 27 February 1979 in Donna, Texas.

► Interviewed on 5 August 1971 in Tehuacana, Texas. Mrs. J. T. Bounds was also present.

► Interviewed by Rich C. Harmon in a studio at Los Angeles radio station KMPC, 26 October 1982.

► Carruthers recorded by John Meredith and Rob Willis at Temora, New South Wales, on 2 December 1990.

► Interviewed 1977, 1978 by Malca Chall. Underwritten by matching grants from the Black Women Oral History Project of the Schlesinger Library on the History of Women, Radcliffe College, by the Columbia Foundation, the Fairtree Foundation, and by friends of Frances Albrier.

► Interviewed by Andrew D. Basiago; 25, 27 September 1985; conference room, University research library, UCLA. This interview was made possible by a grant from the Department of Water and Power, City of Los Angeles.

► Interview conducted by Jeff Anderson, 3 October 1991; recorded and transcribed in German.

► INTERVIEWER: Steven L. Isoardi, UCLA Oral History Program. PLACE: Tape 1 at Douglass's office at the American Federation of Musicians Local 47, Los Angeles; tapes 2–5 at Douglass's home, Los Angeles. DATES, LENGTH OF SESSIONS: February 2, 1990 (77 minutes); February 10, 1990 (129 minutes); February 17, 1990 (76 minutes); March 3, 1990 (69 minutes). TOTAL NUMBER OF RECORDED HOURS: 5.85. PERSONS PRESENT DURING INTERVIEW: Douglass and Isoardi.
(A structured note, employing introductory wording to separate subelements within it, a style devised by the repository)

Oral history projects and collections

Rule: **Give, as a minimum, the following information:**
- **date(s) during which collection or project interviews were undertaken**   √ Fundamental information
- **name(s) or characterization(s) of interviewer(s)**
- **language of the interviews, if other than English**

Rule: *Optionally*, give also the following information:

- sponsorship and/or source of funding
- circumstances applying to all interviews in the collection or project, including type of preparation
- place(s) where interviews were conducted

► Interviews conducted by students enrolled in a class in oral history at Immaculate Heart College, Los Angeles, under the supervision of Knox Mellon, 1973.

► Interviews were conducted 1968–1976 for the Combined Asian American Resource Project (CARP) by students under the direction of Frank Chinn.
(Interviewers characterized rather than named)

► Recorded in Nanticoke, Wilkes-Barre, Hazleton, and other nearby towns in Northeastern Pennsylvania during 1977 and 1978. The project was started and conducted by James P. Rodechko, a professor of history at Wilkes College, Wilkes-Barre, Pennsylvania, and five students (Angela Staskavage, Susan Donio, Kenneth Hughes, Maggie Shaw, and Tom Donahue) in cooperation with the Pennsylvania Historical and Museum Commission (PHMC). Student interviewers received a checklist of procedures for their interviews as well as a question list created by the PHMC of over 80 questions for interviewees.
(Interviewers named; interview preparation noted; place of interviews given)

► This project was funded by the National Endowment for the Humanities and conducted from July 1, 1975, to March 31, 1977, by the UCLA Oral History Program. The project was directed jointly by Page Ackerman, university librarian, and Gerald Nordland, director, UCLA Art Galleries, and administered by Bernard Galm, director, Oral History Program. After selection of interview candidates and interviewers, the UCLA Oral History Program assumed responsibility for the conduct of all interviews and their processing.

► Interviews conducted during 1982 and 1983. INTERVIEWERS: David A. Rose, free-lance consultant, and Rich C. Harmon, editor, Oral History Program, UCLA. INTERVIEWEES: William C. Ackerman, Byron H. Atkinson, James Bush, Robert A. Fischer, Thomas Jacobs, William Nicholas, Thomas Hamilton, David Saxon, Richard Perry, Fred Hessler, Charles Young, Wiles Hallock, and J. Thompson Prothro, Jr.
(A structured note, employing introductory wording to separate subelements within it; style devised by the repository. Alternatively, if the repository chose to give separate descriptions for each of the interviews, the interviewers's names would be more appropriately given in the individual interview records, and it would not be necessary to name each of the interviewers in the description of the project.)

2.7B3   Scope and content/Abstract
AACR 2   1.7B1, 1.7B17
APPM   1.7B2

Individual oral history interviews

✓ Fundamental
information

Rule: **Give information relating to the general content, nature, and scope of the interview.**

Usage note: This may include, but is not limited to:
- geographic area discussed
- names of persons discussed
- time period covered
- summary of subject content: description of events, conditions, objects, and activities, with locations and dates when possible
- opinions and attitudes expressed by the informant
- opinions the informant has heard expressed about the informant or others
- personal recollections about other people
- brief indication of the subject matter of illustrative stories and anecdotes

Not all of this information will be readily available to the cataloger. The repository or the individual cataloger must decide which available information to use and whether any information would be useful enough to justify seeking it when it is not readily available. A primary consideration would be value to users by providing the best context for a particular interview or set of interviews.

While the general content of this note is specified, the repository and the individual cataloger have considerable freedom to decide on the length, amount of detail, and form or style used, as demonstrated in the examples below.

► P. O. McAllister discusses his life and his work at Sloss Furnace (Birmingham, Ala.) as the assistant controller and purchasing coordinator from 1938 to 1958.

► The Minot's Ledge Lighthouse (off the coast of Cohasset, Mass.) and the life of a lighthouse keeper's family during the 1920s and 1930s.

► Haldeman discusses his early life, education, and military service; his involvement in public service organizations and activities; and his partisan political interests. He also discusses his leadership of the UCLA Alumni Association, the origins and development of the UCLA Foundation, and business before the regents during his brief service on the board.

► The interview proceeds chronologically, beginning with Douglass's childhood and education in Texas and Los Angeles and continuing through his career as a jazz musician. Major topics covered include fellow jazz musicians, musical styles, desegregation of jazz groups, the American Federation of Musicians, and the rise and decline of Central Avenue.

► Papa Susso, griot from Gambia, talks about the history of the griot in Gambia and his instrument, the Kora. Year, place of birth, Gambia; message to black community in America about their culture; role of griot in West African society (arrange marriages, settle disputes); change in griot's social condition over history; relationship of griot with kings in Africa; passing information across generations of griots; Alex Haley's visit with griot in Gambia when researching *Roots*; teaching son to be griot, the history and music; ceremony performed once qualified as griot; history of griot tradition and Kora; materials used to manufacture Kora; tuning a Kora; performance of piece composed by Susso's father for Papa Susso and his wife and one about the visit to Schomburg.

► Buchanan describes his work in artificial intelligence, the development of the Stanford Artificial Intelligence Laboratory and the artificial intelligence (AI) community, and the role of the Information Processing Techniques Office of the Advanced Research Projects Agency (later the Defense Advanced Research Projects Agency) in AI research. Buchanan describes the work of Ed Feigenbaum, Josh Lederburg, and Wes Churchman at Stanford, and Les Ernest. He discusses changes in AI funding, including developing additional NIH funding, with the Mansfield amendment which stipulated defense-supported research should have defense applications. Buchanan concludes with a comparison of artificial intelligence and computer science development.

Oral history projects and collections

Rule: **Give information relating to the general content, nature, and scope of the interviews in the collection or project.**

√ Fundamental information

Usage note: This may include, but is not limited to:
- names or characterizations of interviewees
- geographic area(s) discussed or represented
- time period covered
- topics and events documented
- points of view expressed

► Interviews with five residents of Sanpete County, Utah, in which they discuss early twentieth-century life in that area.

► The founding and development of an important New York law firm, with accounts from two of the founding partners and several other members of the firm.

► Creation and development of radio station WOR from several viewpoints; accounts deal with broadcast news, trade-unions, program innovations, music, technical developments, and the effects of blacklisting.

▶ The Earl Warren Era Project (1969–1979) documents the executive branch, the legislature, criminal justice, and political campaigns during the Warren Era in California. Focusing on the years 1925–1953, the interviews also provide a record of the changes wrought in California by successive Depression, war, and postwar boom.

▶ The interviews document construction of a controversial high-voltage electric transmission line across Minnesota farmland. The oral history project was recorded over a three-year period (1977–1979) during the height of the controversy and includes interviews with persons representing major opposing positions. Among them are farmers, state legislators, power company officials, a county sheriff, powerline supporters, and organizers of major opposition groups.

▶ Residents of Alabama who were subjects of the 1941 book, *Let Us Now Praise Famous Men*, by James Agee and Walker Evans, discuss their lives during the Great Depression and since the book was written.

▶ This series of interviews with Pew scholars in the biomedical sciences was conducted by the UCLA Oral History Program in conjunction with the Pew Charitable Trusts' Pew Scholars in the Biomedical Sciences Oral History and Archives Project. The project has been designed to document the backgrounds, education, and research of biomedical scientists awarded five-year Pew scholarships from 1988 through 1992.

▶ The American Indian Oral History Project, 1967–1972, was designed to provide a record of oral traditions by and for the Native American people. Universities from seven states were involved in the project, funded by the Doris Duke Foundation.

▶ Interviews conducted with residents of Jenkins, a former coal company town in eastern Kentucky, to augment the 3,600 photographs in the William R. "Pictureman" Mullins collection. The photographs were taken by Mullins in Jenkins from the late 1930s to the early 1950s. Interviewees include residents portrayed in the photographs.

▶ Interviews with scientists on a wide variety of topics in physics and allied sciences. Areas covered extensively include radio astronomy; high energy physics theory, experiments, and accelerators; fusion energy research; optics, acoustics, and geophysics; physics societies and other organizations; physics education; refugees from fascism; the development of nuclear weapons; physics in industry; and science policy since World War II.

▶ This series of interviews was designed to preserve the spoken memories of individuals, primarily musicians, who were raised near and/or performed on Los Angeles's Central Avenue, especially from the late 1920s to the mid-1950s. Musician and teacher William Green, his student Steven Isoardi, and early project interviewee Buddy Collette provided major inspiration for the UCLA Oral History Program's inaugurating the Central Avenue Sounds Oral History Project.

In preparing for the interview, Isoardi consulted jazz histories, autobiographies, oral histories, relevant jazz periodicals, documentary films, and back issues of the *California Eagle* and the *Los Angeles Sentinel*.

2.7B4   Linking entry complexity
APPM   1.7B3

Individual oral history interviews

✓ Fundamental information

Rule: **If the interview being described was conducted as part of an oral history project, give the title of the project description as formulated under rules 2.1B1–2.1B4. Precede the name of the project with the introductory wording *Forms part of.***

►   Forms part of: Oral history interviews of the Suffragists Oral History Project, 1959–1974

►   Forms part of: Oral history interviews of the State Government Oral History Program

Individual interviews, projects, and collections

Rule: **If the interview, project, or collection being described is a component part or subunit of an archival collection or series that is described separately, give the title of the hierarchically superior unit preceded by the introductory wording *Forms part of.***

►   Forms part of: Richard Critchfield papers, 1953–1986.

►   Forms part of: Duluth Bicentennial Commission records, 1975–1976.

2.7B5   Additional physical form available
AACR 2   1.7B16
APPM   1.7B4

Rule: **Give information about any additional (i.e., different) physical format(s) in which any part of the described material is available for use at the holding repository and/or for loan or purchase.**

If the additional format material is available for distribution, also record availability information (e.g., source, order number, conditions).

Use appropriate introductory wording for subelements when it is necessary to make the nature and intent of their information clear.

► Some transcripts available on microfiche.

► Also available on microfilm: Richard M. Nixon oral history collection, section 3, ch. 4 (Microfilming Corporation of America, 1978).

► Microfiche copy available for purchase; TITLE: Columbia University oral history collection, part IV; AVAILABLE FROM: Meckler Publishing, Westport, Conn.

► Transcript also available in electronic form; 1 computer file (92K); WordPerfect 5.0; copies available on 5-1/4 in. or 3-1/2 in. disk (MS-DOS).

► Transcript also available in electronic form. URL: gopher: // gopher.wheaton.edu /70
> *(In MARC, electronic locations are provided for in a new field 856. It is an unresolved question, therefore, whether electronic availability should be treated in the Additional physical form available note, which is generally associated with MARC field 530.)*

2.7B6   Reproduction
APPM   1.7B5

Rule: **Give information to indicate that the unit of description is a copy of originals that either are located elsewhere or have been destroyed. Give the following elements of information (in order and if available):**
- **type of reproduction**
- **place of reproduction**
- **agency responsible for the reproduction**
- **date of the reproduction**
- **physical description of the reproduction**
- **indication that originals were destroyed after copying, or are otherwise known or suspected to be no longer extant**

Use appropriate introductory wording for individual elements when it is necessary to make the nature and intent of the information clear.

► The tapes and transcript are copies made in 1989.

► The tapes and transcript are copies acquired in 1986.

> ▶ Photocopy.
> *(In all cases, it would be desirable also to give information about who made the copies, if known; and the location of originals, if known. See also* Location of originals/ duplicates, rule 2.7B7, page 48.)

2.7B7   Location of originals/duplicates
APPM   1.7B6

Rule: **Location of originals. If the unit of description consists of re-productions or duplicates, give information to identify any re-positor(ies),** *other than the cataloging repository,* **with custody of the originals. Information may include the name of the cus-todian repository, its address, the country in which it is lo-cated, and its telephone number. Use appropriate introductory wording (e.g.,** *Originals held by:).*

> ▶ Originals held by: Menlo Park Historical Association, Menlo Park, California.

> ▶ Originals at: Oral History Research Office, Columbia Univer-sity, New York, N.Y.

> ▶ Originals in possession of: Oral History of Iran Archives.

> ▶ The original tapes and transcript are held by the Benton County Historical Society.

> ▶ Original of Friedan interview is in the Smith College Archives.

> ▶ Location of originals unknown.

Usage note: For sound recordings and videorecordings, interpret *original* to mean original field recording (i.e., that came from the recording machine used during the interview).

Rule: **Location of duplicates.** *Optionally,* **give the names and address-es of repositories,** *other than the cataloging repository,* **that hold copies—for example, when the cataloging repository controls the distribution of copies and the number of copies is limited.**

> ▶ Copies of the transcripts deposited in: Illinois State Historical Library, Springfield, Ill.

> ▶ Copies at Hunter College.

> ▶ A duplicate set of transcripts has been divided according to the counties of residence of the interviewees and housed at the appropriate area research center: River Falls, Green Bay, Mil-waukee, Stevens Point, and Northland.

2.7B8   Provenance

APPM   1.7B9

Rule: **If the unit of description consists of materials created outside the cataloging repository and transferred to or deposited in the repository, give information (including dates, if available) concerning successive transfers of ownership and custody of the materials.**

►   Professor Herbert Gutman, project director, donated the tapes of the New York City Immigrant Labor Oral History Project to the Robert F. Wagner Labor Archives in 1983. They were transferred from the New Jersey Historical Commission where they had been temporarily housed.

2.7B9   Immediate source of acquisition

APPM   1.7B10

Rule: **Give information concerning the donor or source (i.e., the immediate prior custodian) of the material being cataloged. This information may include:**
* **name of source**
* **address of source**
* **method of acquisition (e.g., gift, purchase, deposit, transfer)**
* **date of the acquisition**
* **accession number(s)**
* **purchase price**
* **relation of the source to the material**

►   Gift of Sandra Taylor, University of Utah department of history, 1988.

►   Purchased from the Regional Oral History Office of the Bancroft Library, University of California, Berkeley, 1991.

►   Gift of Flying Tigers Association.

►   Contributed by the Schlesinger Library, Radcliffe College, Cambridge, MA.

►   Presented by Jean Saul Rannells, Madison, Wis., 1984–1985.

If the source is unknown, give that information.

For materials acquired from multiple sources, make multiple notes, specifying, if desired, materials received in each acquisition.

Usage note: This information may or may not be required by users to evaluate or collocate materials—thus it may or may not be required in a description available to the public (e.g., catalog record). For various reasons, it may be suitable for internal use only. The repository must decide which information, and how much information, about acquisition should be available to users.

2.7B10 Restrictions on access

AACR 2   1.7B20
APPM   1.7B11

√ Fundamental information

Rule: **Give information about any restrictions imposed on access to the interviews. Specify the terms of the restriction, including the date when it will be lifted, if applicable.**

Rule: ***Optionally*, give additional information concerning:**
  - **jurisdiction (i.e., the person, institution, or position or function through which the terms governing access are imposed, enforced, and may be appealed)**
  - **physical access provisions**
  - **authorized users (i.e., individuals or a class of users to whom the restrictions do not apply)**
  - **authorization (i.e., the source of the authority for the restriction).**

  ►   Available for research use at the Charles Babbage Institute only.

  ►   A portion of interview number 3 is sealed until 2020.

  ►   Access restricted until 31 December 2005. Permission for earlier access may be requested through the Minnesota Historical Society.

  ►   Access to portions of this interview, sessions 7 through 9 generating tapes 11 through 17 and transcript pages 393 through 658, is restricted until 1 January 2000 without written permission of interviewee.

  ►   Portions sealed. These are not available for public access until 1 July 2008, except with prior written approval of the interviewee.

  ►   Stored off site; 24-hour advance notice required for use.

Usage note: Repositories may decide the length, amount of detail, and form or style used. Many repositories adopt their own standard wording for various types of restrictions notes.

2.7B11 Terms governing use and reproduction

AACR 2   1.7B20
APPM   1.7B12

Rule: **Give information about terms governing the use of the interview after access has been provided. This includes, but is not** limited to, copyrights, film rights, trade restrictions, etc., that restrict the right to reproduce, exhibit, fictionalize, quote, etc. If the literary rights in interviews were dedicated or reserved under previous copyright law, record that information.

► Copyright held by interviewee.

► Permission of the repository required to cite, quote, or reproduce.

► This transcript is hereby made available for research purposes only. All literary rights in the manuscript, including the right to publication, are reserved to the University Library of the University of California at Los Angeles.

► The interviewee retains copyright to the video and audio tapes and transcripts until 5 February 1999. Until then, scholars may view and listen to the tapes, but must apply to the interviewee to use the materials in any way for public presentation or publication. No copies of the video and audio tapes may be made.

► No part of the interview may be quoted for publication without the written permission of the California State Archivist or the head, Department of Special Collections, University Research Library, UCLA.

Rule: *Optionally*, give information relating to jurisdiction, authorization, and authorized users as for restrictions on access, rule 2.7B10, above.

2.7B12 Cumulative index/finding aids
APPM   1.7B13

Rule: Give information about the presence of any related materials that provide administrative and intellectual controls over the described materials. These may include, but are not limited to, abstracts, tables of contents, and indexes.

► Name and subject index filed with transcript.

► Tape abstract available.

► Name index available.

► Transcripts have been indexed.

► Card index keyed to subjects, names, and tribes available in the repository.

► Finding aids include a computer index, accession book and cards, and donor cards.

► Alphabetical name and numerical interview indexes available. Each interview has a table of contents and index.

► Unpublished finding aid available in repository. Videorecording is linked to finding aid by time coding.

► A preface and table of contents in English are bound with the interview transcript (which is in German).

► Abstracts of some interviews available.

► Case file includes copies of interviewee biographies and abstracts of the interviews, plus a table that identifies interviewees by ethnic group, religion, and occupation, as well as other information.

2.7B13 Citation
AACR 2 1.7B15
APPM 1.7B14

Rule: **Give a brief bibliographic citation[1] for reference to works (other than finding aids specified in rule 2.7B12) in which abstracts, citations, descriptions, calendars, or indexes of the described interviews have appeared. Include journal articles describing portions of the materials and guides describing interviews in terms of a particular subject focus. Use appropriate introductory wording (e.g., *Described in:, Listed in:*) in order to clarify the nature of the citation.**

► Listed in: Holman, Barbara D. Oral history collection of the Forest History Society: an annotated guide.

► Further description of the untranscribed tapes and how they were utilized by Young may be found in: Young, Karl E. Ordeal in Mexico. Salt Lake City: Deseret Book Company, 1968.

Rule: ***Optionally,* give information on the exact location within the source.**

► Described in: Guide to Manuscript Collections in the Sangamon State University Archives, p. 31.

2.7B14 Preferred citation of described materials
APPM 1.7B15

Rule: **Give the format and content for the citation of the described material that is preferred by the repository. Use the introductory phrase *Cite as:* to introduce the citation form.**

► Cite as: William E. Forbes, Oral History Interview, conducted 1990 by Dale E. Treleven, UCLA Oral History Program, for the California State Archives State Government Oral History Program.

---

[1] Citations given in rules 2.7B13, 2.7B14, and 2.7B15 generally follow bibliographic forms recommended in the Chicago Manual of Style, 13th ed. (Chicago: University of Chicago Press, 1982). Repositories may wish to use other forms based on alternate recommendations in Chicago Manual of Style or in AACR 2 (e.g., rule 1.7A4).

▶ Cite as: Dorothea May Moore Oral History. Schlesinger Library, Radcliffe College.

▶ Cite as: Henry O. Holocaust Testimony (HVT-942). Fortunoff Video Archive for Holocaust Testimonies, Yale University Library.

▶ Cite as: American Indian Oral History Collection, Center for Southwest Research, General Library, University of New Mexico.

2.7B15 Publications
APPM 1.7B16

Rule: **Give a citation to or information about a work that is based on the use, study, or analysis of the interviews (e.g., historical studies, biographies, statistical reports). If necessary, use appropriate introductory wording (e.g., *Publications:* or *Portions published in:*) in order to clarify the nature of the citation.**

▶ Publications: Towner, Ann Sibley. "The Attenuation of Community Voluntary Associations and Cultural Change in Brea, California, 1920s–1970s." Master's thesis, California State University, Fullerton, 1985.

▶ Research from this interview (along with two other interviews and a background paper) forms the basis for Laura Anne Oakes's bachelor honors thesis (at James Madison University), "Drugs in the Valley: The History of the Stonewall Plant of Merck and Company, Inc., 1941–1991."

▶ Transcripts of these interviews became a basis for the report: Demetrios Caraley. New York City's Deputy Mayor, City Administrator—Accomplishments, Problems, and Potentialities.

Usage note: Note the difference between works *based on* the interview(s) (cited here) and works in which the interviews have been *described, indexed*, etc., (covered in the citation note, 2.7B13). The difference, though subtle, has implications for USMARC tagging.

2.7B16 General note
APPM 1.7B17

Rule: **Give any other descriptive information considered important but not falling within the definitions of the other notes.**

Physical description

▶ Tape reels transferred from original acetate discs.

▶ Preservation, working duplicate, and cassette copies made.

▶ Lending copy: 1 cassette.

▶ Dubbed from tapes in the Yale Oral History Archives.

► Half-hour interview with Nevins (1963) conducted by Owen Bombard on film, subsequently transferred to 3/4-inch video cassette.

► Text files on disk were prepared using *Write Now* software on a Macintosh computer.

Supplementary materials

► Filed with the transcript are 6 photographs.

► Accompanied by recorded speeches and music from a reunion of Textile Workers Union of America activists and staff in 1984; included is a speech by Alexander E. Barkan and textile labor songs by Joe Glazer.

► Appended to transcript: "Now it can be told," a selection of unpublished sketches.

► Supplementary materials: Chronology of events, damage estimates, and a map showing the path of the storm through the village, all issued by the Barneveld Village Hall.

Relationships to other materials and other catalog records

► Each interviewee's oral history individually cataloged.

► Bound in: Pipelines to the Past: An Oral History of Olinda, California, 1979. 148 p.

Missing information

► Some of the tapes have been erased; only five-minute excerpts remain.

► In 1987 two interviews of the original 55 were determined to be missing (tapes 4 and 15).

► The interviewees in this project were never identified by name—on the tapes or in any associated materials.

Transcripts ("states," versions, editorial changes)

► Transcript incomplete.

► Transcript heavily edited.

Other general information

► The interviewee made minor emendations to the transcript and added some information in writing, Mar.–June 1991.

► Audio tape shelved separately as T-224.

► Participants and pagination: Oscar Bernstien, 79; Paul Crowell, 40; Clarence de la Chapelle, 56; Henry P. Dolan, 76; Clifford Evans, 141; George J. Joyce, 45; Solomon Klein, 160; John J. Lynch, 98; Paul O'Dwyer, 245, permission required; William O'Dwyer, 1,783, permission required.

Usage note: Cataloging rules cannot provide for *every* situation. This permissive rule gives the repository and the cataloger freedom to adapt to particular circumstances. They may provide any additional information they consider important, in the form and style they choose.

CHAPTER 3

CHOICE OF ACCESS POINTS

3.0   INTRODUCTORY RULES

3.0A   Main and added entries

AACR 2   21.0A
APPM   2.0A

> This chapter contains rules for determining some of the access points—namely, personal and corporate name headings and title headings—under which a description might be entered in a catalog or index. (Some people might refer to the process of assigning access points as *indexing*.)

> The access point that is considered primary becomes the *main entry* heading, while the others are designated *added entry* headings.

> The *form* of an entry heading is determined by extensive rules given both in *APPM* (chapters 3–6) and *AACR 2* (chapters 22–25). These rules, which are not repeated in this manual, govern such matters as the order of words in headings, treatment of compound surnames and forenames used alone, and the addition of birth and death dates to some personal name headings.

> Guidelines for determining topical, chronological, form/genre, and geographical access points are not given in this manual.

3.0B   Sources for determining access points

AACR 2   21.0B
APPM   2.0B

Rule: Determine access points from the same sources of information used for the description as a whole (as specified in rule 2.0B). All access points should be justified in the description to which they relate.

Usage note: For any access point, it should be possible to tell from the description how the person or corporate body named in the access point heading relates to the unit of description.

3.1   Basic rule for entry
AACR 2   21.1A2, 21.1B2
APPM   2.1

Rule: **Enter a body of oral history material under the heading for
               the name of the person or corporate body chiefly responsible
               for the creation of the material and its intellectual content, as
               defined in the following rules.**

Usage note: Choice of entry depends on whether the unit of description consists
               of :
               - an interview (or sequence of related interviews) with an
                 individual person
               - a set of interviews created as the product of an oral history
                 project
               - a collection of interviews not associated with a project, but
                 assembled as a group at some time after their creation, usually
                 without regard to their provenance (similar to the *artificial
                 collection* defined in *APPM*)
               - a repository's entire holdings of oral history materials

               In any case, it is always important to make clear the relationship
               between the person or organization named in the main entry head-
               ing (if there is one) and any added entry headings and the unit be-
               ing described. Use the interview details note (rule 2.7B2) to clarify
               the relationships if the headings (with any relator terms) and title
               alone are not sufficient.

3.1A   Oral history interviews with individuals

3.1A1   Oral history interview(s) with a single individual—*entry under the heading for the name of the individual*
AACR 2   21.6, esp. 21.6B
APPM   2.1A6

Rule: **Enter an interview or a sequence of related interviews with a
               single individual under the heading for the interviewee. Follow
               the heading with the relator term *interviewee*.**

               ► Harris, Myrtle, interviewee.
                 Oral history interview with Myrtle Harris, 1974.

               ► Oppenheim, Adelaide, interviewee.
                 Oral history interview with Adelaide Oppenheim, 1976.

               ► Booth, Cameron, interviewee.
                 Oral history interviews with Cameron Booth, 1971, 1977.

               ► Hall, S. Edward, 1878–1975, interviewee.
                 Oral history interviews with S. Edward Hall, 1970–1974.

Make an added entry for each interviewer, as specified in rule 3.3C.

Usage note: Although an oral history interviewer generally initiates the interview and often influences its direction, the interviewee is considered chiefly responsible for the informational content and narrative style of the interview.

Rule: **If the name of the interviewee is unknown, enter the description under title.**

► Oral history interview with a North Dakota homesteader, 1956.

Usage note: This should be extremely uncommon, since oral history practice manuals and guidelines all specify the name of the interviewer as essential information.

3.1A2 **Oral history interviews with two or more individuals—***entry under the heading for name of the predominant participant, or under title*
APPM   2.1A6

Rule: **If the unit being cataloged consists of an interview or sequence of interviews in which two or more persons were present and actively participating, enter the unit either**
- **under the heading for the person whose comments predominate, or**
- **under title,** *if no individual predominates.*

Make added entries for all interviewees not named in the main entry (see Two or more interviewees, rule 3.3A, page 63).

► Perrizo, Rose Hughes, interviewee.
        Oral history interview with Rose Hughes Perrizo and Anne Hughes, 1977.
            (If it is known that Perrizo's comments predominate, enter under Perrizo and make added entry for Hughes.)

► Johnson, Hilfred, 1906– , interviewee.
        Oral history interview with Hilfred Johnson and Lester Pollard, 1976.
            (If it is known that Johnson's comments predominate, enter under Johnson and make added entry for Pollard.)

► Oral history interview with Mark Strong and Gail Watkins, 1978.
            (If it is known that neither person's comments predominate, enter under title and make added entries for both Strong and Watkins.)

Usage note: Most manuals and guidelines for oral history discourage interviewing more than one person at a time, but it does occur in certain circumstances.

3.1B   Oral history project interviews—*entry under the heading for the project*

Rule: **If the unit of description consists of interviews undertaken as part of a project, enter the description under the heading for the project as a corporate body.**

Usage note: According to *AACR 2* rule 21.1B1, consider a named project to be a corporate body. Consider a project to have a name if it is consistently given as a proper noun (in English, spelled with initial capitals) in project documentation such as correspondence, deeds of gift, and grant proposals. Projects often have their own offices, staff, or letterhead.

In this situation, the project is considered to be chiefly responsible (in the sense of archival provenance) for the creation of the project interviews *considered as a whole.*

►   Suffragists Oral History Project.
      Oral history interviews of the Suffragists Oral History Project, 1959–1974.
      (Construct the heading for the project as a corporate body according to AACR 2 chapter 24 or APPM rules Chapter 5)

►   Medical College of Pennsylvania. Oral History Project on Women in Medicine.
      Oral history interviews of the Medical College of Pennsylvania Oral History Project on Women in Medicine, 1977–1978.

►   Northwest Oral History Project.
      Oral history interviews of the Northwest Oral History Project, 1982–1985.

►   Smithsonian Institution Oral History Project.
      Oral history interviews of the Smithsonian Institution Oral History Project, ca. 1970–[ongoing].

►   Barneveld Tornado Oral History Project.
      Oral history interviews of the Barneveld Tornado Oral History Project, 1984.

►   Eleanor Roosevelt Oral History Project (Franklin D. Roosevelt Library)
      Oral history interviews of the Eleanor Roosevelt Oral History Project, 1977–1980.

►   Last Battleship Oral History Project.
      Oral history interviews of The Last Battleship Oral History Project, 1988.

3.1C   Collection of oral history interviews not associated with a project—*entry under name of individual collector or under title*

Rule: **If the unit of description is a collection that is known primarily by its association with a particular individual collector (e.g., an independent researcher or other person who brought the materials together), enter the description under the heading for the name of the collector. Follow the heading with the term** *collector.*

Usage note: Use the term *collector* in the main entry heading even if the collector also functioned as interviewer. Do not treat any corporate body as a collector.

 ►   Durr, Virginia Foster, collector.
         Virginia Durr oral history collection, 1988.

 ► · Hatch, James Vernon, 1928– , collector.
         Hatch-Billops oral history collection of interviews with African-American dancers and choreographers, 1971–1974.

Rule: **If the unit of description is a collection that is not associated with an individual collector, or if such an association cannot be determined, enter it under title.**

 ►   Kentucky history oral history collection, 1977–[ongoing]
         (Miscellaneous interviews relating in some way to Kentucky history, but not created as part of any project)

3.1D   Repository's entire holdings—*entry under the heading for the name of the repository*

Rule: **If the unit of description consists of the** *entire* **oral history holdings of a single repository, enter it under the heading for the name of the repository.**

Usage note: In this case, the repository as a whole is considered chiefly responsible (again in the sense of archival provenance) for the creation of the holdings, which represents the activity of the repository in the collection and administration of oral history materials.

 ►   Port Washington Public Library (Port Washington, N.Y.)
         Oral history collection of Port Washington Public Library, 1980–1989.

 ►   Greenup County Public Library. South Shore Branch.
         Oral history collection of the Greenup County Public Library, South Shore Branch (Kentucky), 1976–1981.

 ►   Charles Dawson History Center (White Plains, N.Y.)
         Oral history collection of the Charles Dawson History Center, 1972–1988.

► Friars of the Atonement. Archives.
   Oral history collection of the Friars of the Atonement Archives, 1986–1988.

► Ford Foundation. Archives.
   Oral history collection of the Ford Foundation Archives, 1975–1986.

► Chase Manhattan Corporation. Archives.
   Oral history collection of the Chase Manhattan Corporation Archives, 1960–1987.

3.1E   Collections of uncertain origin—*entry under title*

Rule: **If it cannot be determined that the unit of description clearly falls into one of the categories in rules 3.1A–3.1D, enter it under title.**

3.1F   Project name change
         APPM   2.1B3

Rule: **If the name of an oral history project has changed over the period of time covered by the interviews being described, enter the description under the heading for the last name represented in the materials. If the name changes and the project continues, change the main entry heading to reflect the newer name. Make an added entry under the heading for each predecessor name represented.**

Added Entries

3.2   GENERAL RULES
       AACR 2 21.29
       APPM   2.2

Rule: **Make added entries, as specified below, to provide access to descriptions in addition to the access provided by the main entry heading.**

3.2A   Alternate entries likely to be sought by catalog users
         AACR 2 21.29C, 21.29D
         APPM   2.2C, 2.2D

Rule: **Make an added entry under the heading for a person or a corporate body or under a title if some catalog users might suppose that the description of the material/item would be found under that heading or title rather than under the heading or title chosen for the main entry.**

> American Indian oral history interviews
> *(Project well known to have been funded by Doris Duke; sometimes known as the Duke Collection; make an added personal name entry for Doris Duke and an added title entry for the Duke Collection.)*

Rule: **If, in the context of a given catalog, an added entry is required under a heading or title other than those prescribed below, make it.**

Usage note: Most of the rules in this chapter are intended to deal with the types of access points (added entry headings) most commonly required. Because it would be impossible to anticipate all possible circumstances, this rule is intentionally permissive. Catalogers should exercise judgment in unusual cases to provide other access points for users.

3.2B Form of headings

AACR 2   21.29E
APPM   2.2E

Rule: **Construct a heading for an added entry according to the instructions in *APPM* chapters 3–6 (*AACR 2* chapters 22–25).**

Usage note: The rules in *APPM/AACR 2* are extensive, and the kinds of name headings required for oral history cataloging are not different from those used in cataloging other materials, so catalogers should use one of the recommended existing tools for this purpose.

3.2C Added entries must be justified in the description

AACR 2   21.29F
APPM   2.2F

Rule: **Be certain that the name of the person or body or the title in an added entry is either given specifically or characterized somewhere in the description (including notes).**

Usage note: The description for an oral history project might contain the names of the individual interviewees involved. If there are very many, the description might characterize them as, for example, "interviewees were residents of Jenkins, a former coal company town in eastern Kentucky." Added entries for persons might therefore be assumed to be residents of Jenkins.

3.3   SPECIFIC RULES

3.3A   Two or more interviewees
APPM   2.3A1

Rule: **If the main entry for an oral history interview with two or more active participants is entered under the heading for the predominant interviewee, make an added entry under the heading for each of the other interviewees. Follow each heading with the relator term** *interviewee.*

3.3B   Project interviewees

Rule: *Optionally,* **for the description of an oral history project, make an added entry for any or all persons interviewed as part of the project. Follow each heading with the relator term** *interviewee.*

Usage note: If the individual interviews that are part of a project are cataloged separately, there is probably no need in the description of the project to make an added entry for each interviewee.

3.3C   Interviewers
APPM   2.1A6

Rule: **For the descriptions of an oral history interview (or sequence of interviews) with an individual, make an added entry under the heading for the person(s) responsible for conducting the interview. Follow the heading with the relator term** *interviewer.*

►   Nelson, Edward, interviewer

Usage note: Standard oral history practice involves a single interviewer with a single interviewee, but there may be instances in which different persons interviewed the same person as part of a long-term project.

Rule: *Optionally,* **for the description of an oral history project or collection, make an added entry under the heading for any or all interviewers.**

Usage note: If a large project involved many interviewers, it probably is not necessary to make an added entry for every interviewer. In such a case, consider making added entries only for interviewers who 1) contributed significantly to the development of the project; 2) conducted a significant number of interviews; 3) wrote monographs based on the interviews conducted; or 4) are considered prominent or "well known," if this information can be determined readily. Also, if the individual interviews are cataloged separately, there is probably no need in the description of the project to have added entries for the interviewers.

3.3D   Corporate bodies associated with an oral history project or collection
AACR 2   21.30E

Rule: **If the unit of description is an oral history project or collection, make an added entry under the heading for any corporate body associated with it—if that name is thought to be required for access.**

►   The project was started and conducted by James P. Odechko, a professor of history at Wilkes College, Wilkes-Barre, Pennsylvania, and five students (Angela Staskavage, Susan Donio, Kenneth Hughes, Maggie Shaw, and Tom Donahue) in cooperation with the Pennsylvania Historical and Museum Commission (PHMC).
     (Interview details note)
     Wilkes College
     Pennsylvania Historical and Museum Commission
       (Added entries)

►   Interviews conducted as a project sponsored by the Foundation for Iranian Studies and Columbia University Oral History Research Office.
     (Part of Interview details note)
     Foundation for Iranian Studies
     Columbia University. Oral History Research Office
       (Added entries)

►   Project sponsored by American Museum of the Moving Image to gather information from people involved with the motion picture industry in New York City.
     (Part of Interview details note)
     American Museum of the Moving Image
       (Added entry)

Usage note: Interpret *associated with* to mean involved in the development or management of the project or collection, including sponsorship or funding.

3.3E   Project names

Rule: **If the unit of description is an individual interview that is part of a named project, make an added entry for the name of the project of which the described materials form a part.**

Usage note: The name of the project also should have been given in a note (see Linking entry complexity, rule 2.7B4, page 46).

The added entry will be the *corporate name heading* for the project (see rule 3.1B).

> ► Suffragists Oral History Project (Bancroft Library)

> ► United States. Commission on the Ukraine Famine. Oral History Project

3.3F Alternate titles

Rule: **Make an added entry for any title, other than that given in the Title area (2.1), by which the material is known.**

> ► Oral history interview with William Douglass
> *(The repository has both tape and transcript and is cataloging them as a unit. The cataloger supplies this title in title area.)*
> Central Avenue sounds—William Douglass
> *(This title, which appears only on the transcript, is given as an added entry.)*

> ► Oral history interviews of the Los Angeles Art Community Oral History Project
> *(The repository has both tapes and transcripts and is cataloging them as a unit. The cataloger supplies this project title in title area.)*
> Los Angeles art community group portrait
> *(This title, which appears only on copies of transcripts for project interviews, is given as an added entry.)*

> ► Oral history interview with Manfredo Tafuri
> *(The repository has both tape and transcript and is cataloging them as a unit. The cataloger supplies title given in title area.)*
> La Storia come progetto
> History as project
> *(These titles in Italian and English, which appear only on the bound transcript, are given as added entries.)*

3.3F1 Titles of songs, poems, etc.

AACR 2 21.30G, 21.30M
APPM 2.3G

Rule: **If a unit of description contains within it, or is related to, an entity that is significant in its own right (e.g., a named song, poem, etc.) and to which the repository wants to provide access, make an added entry (name-title or title, as appropriate) for the entity. Construct the added entry using the same method used to construct the main entry and title of a separate record according to appropriate cataloging rules.**

Usage note: To decide when to make a name-title entry and when to make a title entry, consider how the work would be entered if it were being described by itself instead of as part of something else. In general, if the work has a known author, make a name-title added entry using the heading for the name of the author. If possible, check a library catalog to see how it has been entered there. If in doubt or if authorship information is unavailable, make an added entry for the title alone.

►   Bricky Stratton sings "A Saddle for a Pillow," "My Little Wooden Hut," and "Carolina Rolling Stone," and talks about wheat stacking and rabbiting.
    (Information given in scope and content note)
    Saddle for a pillow
    My little wooden hut
    Carolina rolling stone
    (Title added entries)

►   Residents of Alabama who were subjects of the 1941 book, *Let Us Now Praise Famous Men*, by James Agee and Walker Evans, discuss their lives during the Great Depression and since the book was written.
    (Information given in scope and content note)
    Agee, James, 1909–1955. Let us now praise famous men.
    (Author-title added entry)

Examples

This appendix contains examples of entire descriptions created using the rules in this manual. On facing pages are USMARC-tagged versions of the same records. These examples are based on real descriptions of real records, although in some cases the original descriptions may have been edited for use in this manual.

The records described are held by Minnesota Historical Society (Paul I.V. Strong, Minnesota Farm Advocate Program Oral History Project); Bentley Historical Library (Olga M. Madar); Charles Babbage Institute (Severo Ornstein, Role of DARPA/IPTO in the Development of Computer Science Project); Santa Clara State University (Al Ruffo); Museum of Modern Art (Jeanne C. Thayer); State Historical Society of Wisconsin (Rangnar and Margaret Segerstrom); Schomburg Center for Research in Black Culture (Mother Hale and Dr. Lorraine Hale); Robert Wagner Labor Archives (New York City Immigrant Labor Oral History Project, Hispanic apparel union officers); American Museum of the Moving Image (New York Motion Picture Industry Oral History Project); American Institute of Physics, Neils Bohr Library (General physics topics); Woodstock Library, Woodstock, New York (Woodstock artists); Smithsonian Institution (Black aviators); Greenup County Public Library, South Shore Branch; and Herbert Lehman College (Bronx Institute Archives).

Notes concerning USMARC tagging

These examples are included for illustration only, and cannot be considered authoritative for all circumstances. These examples do not show fixed field tagging, which would be required for a complete USMARC record. They do not show subject headings, which should be assigned from standard lists, such as Library of Congress Subject Headings.

In cases where indicators must be assigned based on the needs of a particular catalog, the indicators have been chosen arbitrarily (e.g., the first indicator in field 245 has always been set to *0*, for "no title added entry"). When an indicator is blank, this is represented by *b̸*. The spacing between content designators and data elements as given here is dictated by the need for typographical clarity; individual systems may have different requirements.

Individual oral history interview

Main entry (Chapter 3)

Ornstein, Severo, interviewee.

Description (chapters 1 and 2)

Oral history interview with Severo Ornstein, 1990 Mar. 6.
Sound recordings: 2 sound cassettes (ca. 60 min. each) : analog, mono.
Transcript : 47 p.
Computer scientist.

Ornstein describes his experience at Lincoln Laboratory, which included work on the SAGE, TX2, and LINC computers. He discusses his involvement with the LINC project, including its move to Washington University, and the later work there on DARPA/IPTO sponsored macromodule project. As the principal hardware designer of the Interface Message Processor (IMP) for the ARPANET, Ornstein describes the IMP design work at Bolt, Beranek and Newman (BBN), the working environment of the group at BBN, his relationship with Lawrence Roberts, his interactions with Honeywell, and his work on the Pluribus multi-processor IMP. Ornstein also discusses the contributions of Wesley Clark and Norman Abramson, his involvement with the Computer Professionals for Social Responsibility, and his views on artificial intelligence and time-sharing.

Interview conducted on 6 March 1991, by Judy E. O'Neill; recorded in Woodside, Calif.

Transcript also available in electronic form: 1 computer file (92K)
If tape used, transcript MUST accompany tape.
Copyright owned by the Charles Babbage Institute.
Forms part of: Oral history interviews of the Role of DARPA/IPTO in the Development of Computer Science Project, 1989–1991.

Added entries (Chapter 3)

O'Neill, Judy E. (Judy Elizabeth), interviewer.
Role of DARPA/IPTO in the Development of Computer Science Project.

Individual oral history interview—USMARC tagging

Rule no.	Tag	Ind.	Field contents
3.1A1	100	1♭	‡a Ornstein, Severo, ‡e interviewee.
2.1A1–2.1A4	245	00	‡a Oral history interview with Severo Ornstein, ‡f 1990 Mar. 6.
2.5C1–2.5C3, 2.5C6, 2.5E	300	♭♭	‡3 Sound recordings: ‡a 2 sound cassettes (ca. 60 min. each) : ‡b analog, mono.
2.5B1, 2.5E	300	♭♭	‡3 Transcript : ‡a 47 p.
2.7B1	545	♭♭	‡a Computer scientist.
2.7B3	520	♭♭	‡b Ornstein describes his experience at Lincoln Laboratory, which included work on the SAGE, TX2, and LINC computers. He discusses his involvement with the LINC project, including its move to Washington University, and the later work there on DARPA/IPTO sponsored macromodule project. As the principal hardware designer of the Interface Message Processor (IMP) for the ARPANET, Ornstein describes the IMP design work at Bolt, Beranek and Newman (BBN), the working environment of the group at BBN, his relationship with Lawrence Roberts, his interactions with Honeywell, and his work on the Pluribus multi-processor IMP. Ornstein also discusses the contributions of Wesley Clark and Norman Abramson, his involvement with the Computer Professionals for Social Responsibility, and his views on artificial intelligence and time-sharing.
2.7B2	500		‡a Interview conducted on 6 March 1991, by Judy E. O'Neill; recorded in Woodside, Calif.
2.7B5	530	♭♭	‡a Transcript also available in electronic form: 1 computer file (92K)
2.7B11	506	♭♭	‡a If tape used, transcript MUST accompany tape.
2.7B11	540	♭♭	‡a Copyright owned by the Charles Babbage Institute.
2.7B4	580	♭♭	‡a Forms part of: Oral history interviews of the Role of DARPA/IPTO in the Development of Computer Science Project, 1989-1991.
3.3C	700	1♭	‡a O'Neill, Judy E. ‡q (Judy Elizabeth), ‡e interviewer.
3.3E	710	2♭	‡a Role of DARPA/IPTO in the Development of Computer Science Project.

Individual oral history interview

Main entry (Chapter 3)

Strong, Paul I. V., interviewee.

Description (chapters 1 and 2)

Oral history interview with Paul I.V. Strong, 1990 Feb. 14.
Sound recordings: 4 sound cassettes (ca. 60 min. each)
Transcript: 79 p. ; 28 cm.

Strong discusses issues related to preservation and management of the loon population in Minnesota and in the U.S. in general. He comments on community action groups, national loon protection associations, and on other avenues of citizen involvement in loon protection efforts.

Strong was born in Augusta, Maine. He received a degree in biology from the University of Maine at Orono and later earned a master's degree in wildlife ecology and a doctorate in wildlife resources from Oklahoma State University. He joined the staff of the Sigurd Olson Environmental Institute at Northland College in Ashland, Wisc., in 1985, serving as coordinator for Wisconsin Project LoonWatch, and later of the Chippewa National Forest in Walker, Minn. He is a trustee of the North American Loon Fund and has published widely in the field of wildlife management.

Interviewed by James E. Fogerty on 14 Feb. 1990 in Walker, Minn.

Forms part of: Minnesota Environmental Issues Oral History Project.

An interview description sheet is available in the repository, filed in the oral history notebooks as OH 139.1.

Added entries (Chapter 3)

Fogerty, James E., 1945– interviewer.
Minnesota Environmental Issues Oral History Project.

Individual oral history interview—USMARC tagging

Rule no.	Tag	Ind.	Field contents
3.1A1	100	1ƀ	‡a Strong, Paul I. V., ‡e interviewee.
2.1A1–2.1A4	245	00	‡a Oral history interview with Paul I.V. Strong, ‡f 1990 Feb. 14.
2.5C1–2.5C2, 2.5E	300	ƀƀ	‡3 Sound recordings: ‡a 4 sound cassettes (ca. 60 min. each)
2.5B1, 2.5B3, 2.5E	300	ƀƀ	‡3 Transcript: ‡a 79 p. ; ‡c 28 cm.
2.7B3	520	0ƀ	‡a Strong discusses issues related to preservation and management of the loon population in Minnesota and in the U.S. in general. He comments on community action groups, national loon protection associations, and on other avenues of citizen involvement in loon protection efforts.
2.7B1	545	ƀƀ	‡a Strong was born in Augusta, Maine. He received a degree in biology from the University of Maine at Orono and later earned a master's degree in wildlife ecology and a doctorate in wildlife resources from Oklahoma State University. He joined the staff of the Sigurd Olson Environmental Institute at Northland College in Ashland, Wisc., in 1985, serving as coordinator for Wisconsin Project LoonWatch, and later of the Chippewa National Forest in Walker, Minn. He is a trustee of the North American Loon Fund and has published widely in the field of wildlife management.
2.7B2	500	ƀƀ	‡a Interviewed by James E. Fogerty on 14 Feb. 1990 in Walker, Minn.
2.7B4	580	ƀƀ	‡a Forms part of: Minnesota Environmental Issues Oral History Project.
2.7B12	555	8ƀ	‡a An interview description sheet is available in the repository, filed in the oral history notebooks as OH 139.1.
3.3C	700	1ƀ	‡a Fogerty, James E., ‡d 1945- ‡e interviewer.
3.3E	710	2ƀ	‡a Minnesota Environmental Issues Oral History Project.

Individual oral history interviews

Main entry (Chapter 3)

Madar, Olga M., interviewee.

Description (chapters 1 and 2)

Oral history interview with Olga M. Madar, [ca. 1971].
1 sound cassette (ca. 90 min.)
Vice-president of the United Auto Workers.
Oral history interview conducted by Patricia Murphy Frank, regarding Madar's role in the Michigan Parks Association.

Added entries (Chapter 3)

Frank, Patricia Murphy, interviewer.

Main entry (chapter 3)

Ruffo, Al, interviewee.

Description (chapters 1 and 2)

Oral history interview with Al Ruffo, 1992 Oct. 1 [videorecording].
1 videocassette (VHS) (66 min.) : col. ; 1/2 in.
Interview with Al Ruffo, past football coach of the Santa Clara Broncos and one of the Santa Clara University Law School's first graduates.
Sponsored by the Bench and Bar Historical Society of Santa Clara County.
Interviewer: Mark Thomas.

Added entries (chapter 3)

Thomas, Mark E., 1930– interviewer.
Bench and Bar Historical Society of Santa Clara County.

Individual oral history interviews—USMARC tagging

Rule no.	Tag	Ind.	Field contents
3.1A1	100	1ƀ	‡a Madar, Olga M., ‡e interviewee.
2.1A–2.1A4	245	00	‡a Oral history interview with Olga M. Madar, ‡f [ca. 1971].
2.5C1–2.5C2	300	ƀƀ	‡a 1 sound cassette (ca. 90 min.)
2.7B1	545	ƀƀ	‡a Vice-president of the United Auto Workers.
2.7B2, 2.7B3	520	0ƀ	‡a Oral history interview conducted by Patricia Murphy Frank, regarding Madar's role in the Michigan Parks Association.
3.3C	700	1ƀ	‡a Frank, Patricia Murphy, ‡e interviewer.

Rule no.	Tag	Ind.	Field contents
3.1A1	100	1ƀ	‡a Ruffo, Al, ‡e interviewee.
2.1A1– 2.1A4, 2.1E	245	00	‡a Oral history interview with Al Ruffo, ‡f 1992 Oct. 1 ‡h [videorecording].
2.5D1–2.1D4	300	ƀƀ	‡a 1 videocassette (VHS) (66 min.) : ‡b col. ; ‡c 1/2 in.
2.7B1, 2.7B3	520	ƀƀ	‡a Interview with Al Ruffo, past football coach of the Santa Clara Broncos and one of the Santa Clara University Law School's first graduates.
2.7B2	500	ƀƀ	‡a Sponsored by the Bench and Bar Historical Society of Santa Clara County.
2.7B2	500	ƀƀ	‡a Interviewer: Mark Thomas.
3.3C	700	1ƀ	‡a Thomas, Mark E., ‡d 1930- ‡e interviewer.
3.3D	710	2ƀ	‡a Bench and Bar Historical Society of Santa Clara County.

Individual oral history interview

Main entry (Chapter 3)

Thayer, Jeanne C., 1917– interviewee.

Description (chapters 1 and 2)

Oral history interview with Jeanne C. Thayer, 1994.
Transcript: 58 p.
Sound recording: 1 sound cassette (ca. 90 min.)
Interview conducted by Sharon Zane for The Museum of Modern Art Oral History Project.

Trustee, The Museum of Modern Art (Oct. 14, 1992–); Ex-Officio Trustee as President of the International Council, 1991– ; Member, Hospitality Committee, 1970–78 (Chairman, 1972–74); Chairman, Special Events Committee, 1973–76; Member, Prints and Illustrated Books, 1980– (Vice-Chairman, 1984–); Member, Painting and Sculpture Committee, 1989–; Co-Chairman, Special Events Committee, 1990– ; Chairman, Conservation Committee, 1993– .

Mrs. Thayer discusses her involvement with the Museum from the late 1960s through 1994, including service on the Hospitality Committee (renamed the Special Events Committee in 1977) and related events, such as the annual Spring Party in the Garden. Other areas chronicled are the use of volunteers in the Museum, Thayer's presidency of the International Council, her participation on the Painting and Sculpture, Print, and Conservation Committee, and her deep interest in modern art.

Forms part of: Museum of Modern Art Oral History Project, 1990–1994.

Gift of Jeanne C. Thayer, 1994.

Transcripts available to qualified users by appointment at Museum of Modern Art Archives and Rockefeller Archive Center. Transcripts with interviewee's notes are not available.

Duplication not permitted.

Name index available.

Original recordings stored at Rockefeller Archive Center.

Duplicate recordings stored at Museum of Modern Art Archives.

Transcripts housed at Rockefeller Archive Center and Museum of Modern Art Archives.

Transcripts with interviewee's notes housed at Rockefeller Archive Center; not available to researchers.

Added entries (Chapter 3)

Museum of Modern Art Oral History Project.
Zane, Sharon.

Individual oral history interview—USMARC tagging

Rule no.	Tag	Ind.	Field contents
3.1A1	100	1b	‡a Thayer, Jeanne C., ‡d 1917- ‡e interviewee.
2.1A1–2.1A4	245	00	‡a Oral history interview with Jeanne C. Thayer, ‡f 1994.
2.5B1, 2.5E	300	bb	‡3 Transcript: ‡a 58 p.
2.5C1–2.5C2, 2.5E	300	bb	‡3 Sound recording: ‡a 1 sound cassette (ca. 90 min.)
2.7B2	500	bb	‡a Interview conducted by Sharon Zane for The Museum of Modern Art Oral History Project.
2.7B1	545	bb	‡a Trustee, The Museum of Modern Art (Oct. 14, 1992-); Ex-Officio Trustee as President of the International Council, 1991- ; Member, Hospitality Committee, 1970-78 (Chairman, 1972-74); Chairman, Special Events Committee, 1973-76; Member, Prints and Illustrated Books, 1980- (Vice-Chairman, 1984-); Member, Painting and Sculpture Committee, 1989- ; Co-Chairman, Special Events Committee, 1990- ; Chairman, Conservation Committee, 1993- .
2.7B3	520	0b	‡a Mrs. Thayer discusses her involvement with the Museum from the late 1960s through 1994, including service on the Hospitality Committee (renamed the Special Events Committee in 1977) and related events, such as the annual Spring Party in the Garden. Other areas chronicled are the use of volunteers in the Museum, Thayer's presidency of the International Council, her participation on the Painting and Sculpture, Print, and Conservation Committee, and her deep interest in modern art.
2.7B4	580	bb	‡a Forms part of: Museum of Modern Art Oral History Project, 1990–1994.
2.7B9	541	bb	‡a Gift of Jeanne C. Thayer, 1994.
2.7B10	506	bb	‡a Transcripts available to qualified users by appointment at Museum of Modern Art Archives and Rockefeller Archive Center. Transcripts with interviewee's notes are not available.
2.7B11	540	bb	‡a Duplication not permitted.
2.7B12	555	bb	‡a Name index available.
2.7B7	535	1b	‡3 Original recordings stored at ‡a Rockefeller Archive Center.
2.7B7	535	2b	‡3 Duplicate recordings stored at ‡a Museum of Modern Art Archives.
2.7B7	535	1b	‡3 Transcripts housed at ‡a Rockefeller Archive Center and Museum of Modern Art Archives.
2.7B7	535	1b	‡3 Transcripts with interviewee's notes housed at ‡a Rockefeller Archive Center; not available to researchers.
3.3C	700	1b	‡a Zane, Sharon, ‡e interviewer.
3.3E	710	2b	‡a Museum of Modern Art Oral History Project.

Individual oral history interview

Main entry (Chapter 3)

Segerstrom, Rangnar, 1896– interviewee.

Description (chapters 1 and 2)

Oral history interview with Rangnar and Margaret Segerstrom, 1976.
6 sound tape reels (ca. 30 min. each)

Interview conducted in 1976 by Dale Treleven of the Historical Society staff with Rangnar and Margaret Segerstrom, retired Mondovi, Wisconsin, dairy farmers; concerning their farming operation between 1922 and 1958; their activities in the Wisconsin Farmers Union, its youth program, and its Central Exchange; membership in other cooperatives and in the Farmers Holiday Association; efforts promoting rural electrification; and the Democratic Party in Buffalo County.

Forms part of: Wisconsin Agriculturalists Oral History Project.

Indexed abstract filed with the registers. Cumulative index to this and other project interviews filed under "Wisconsin Agriculturalists Oral History Project."

Added entries (Chapter 3)

Wisconsin Agriculturalists Oral History Project.
Segerstrom, Margaret, interviewee.
Treleven, Dale, interviewer.

Individual oral history interview—USMARC tagging

Rule no.	Tag	Ind.	Field contents
3.1A2	100	1ƀ	‡a Segerstrom, Rangnar, ‡d 1896- ‡e interviewee.
2.1A1–2.1A4	245	00	‡a Oral history interview with Rangnar and Margaret Segerstrom, ‡f 1976.
2.5C1–2.5C2	300	ƀƀ	‡a 6 sound tape reels (ca. 30 min. each)
2.7B1, 2.7B2, 2.7B3	520	0ƀ	‡a Interview conducted in 1976 by Dale Treleven of the Historical Society staff with Rangnar and Margaret Segerstrom, retired Mondovi, Wisconsin, dairy farmers; concerning their farming operation between 1922 and 1958; their activities in the Wisconsin Farmers Union, its youth program, and its Central Exchange; membership in other cooperatives and in the Farmers Holiday Association; efforts promoting rural electrification; and the Democratic Party in Buffalo County.
2.7B4	580	ƀƀ	‡a Forms part of: Wisconsin Agriculturalists Oral History Project.
2.7B12	555	0ƀ	‡a Indexed abstract filed with the registers. Cumulative index to this and other project interviews filed under "Wisconsin Agriculturalists Oral History Project."
3.3E	710	2ƀ	‡a Wisconsin Agriculturalists Oral History Project.
3.3A	700	1ƀ	‡a Segerstrom, Margaret, ‡e interviewee.
3.3C	700	2ƀ	‡a Treleven, Dale, ‡e interviewer.

Individual oral history interview

Description (chapters 1 and 2)

Oral history interview with Mother Hale and Dr. Lorraine Hale, 1985 June 18 [videorecording].

2 videocassettes (U-Matic) (79 min.) : col. ; 3/4 in.

Interviewed by James Briggs Murray on 18 June 1985 at the Schomburg Center for Research in Black Culture, New York Public Library, New York City.

Clara ("Mother") Hale and Dr. Lorraine Hale are the founders of Hale House in Harlem, N.Y., a temporary home for children of drug-addicted parents.

Mother Hale and Dr. Lorraine Hale talk about drug addiction, the importance of parental roles, Hale House and its children, and their philosophy of life. (1) Early life and how she got into child care; Lorraine Hale's accomplishments; importance of American identity; drug addiction; origins of Hale House; sources of funding; philosophy of Hale House; caring for babies going through withdrawal; children's needs and the importance of parental authority; common-sense guidelines offered to parents; drug epidemics; Hale House hotline; Percy Sutton's help; (2) Oval Office visit and impressions of Ronald Reagan; philosophy of life; Conference on the Innocent Child; philosophy of work.

Permission required to cite, quote, and reproduce; contact repository for information.

Added entries (Chapter 3)

Hale, Clara, d. 1992, interviewee.
Hale, Lorraine, interviewee.
Murray, James Briggs, interviewer.

Individual oral history interview—USMARC tagging

Rule no.	Tag	Ind.	Field contents
2.1A1–2.1A4, 3.1A2, 2.1E	245	00	‡a Oral history interview with Mother Hale and Dr. Lorraine Hale, ‡f 1985 June 18 ‡h [videorecording].
2.5D1–2.5D4	300	ƀƀ	‡a 2 videocassettes (U-Matic) (79 min.) : ‡b col. ; ‡c 3/4 in.
2.7B2	500	ƀƀ	‡a Interviewed by James Briggs Murray on 18 June 1985 at the Schomburg Center for Research in Black Culture, New York Public Library, New York City.
2.7B1	545	ƀƀ	‡a Clara ("Mother") Hale and Dr. Lorraine Hale are the founders of Hale House in Harlem, N.Y., a temporary home for children of drug-addicted parents.
2.7B3	520	0ƀ	‡a Mother Hale and Dr. Lorraine Hale talk about drug addiction, the importance of parental roles, Hale House and its children, and their philosophy of life. ‡b (1) Early life and how she got into child care; Lorraine Hale's accomplishments; importance of American identity; drug addiction; origins of Hale House; sources of funding; philosophy of Hale House; caring for babies going through withdrawal; children's needs and the importance of parental authority; common-sense guidelines offered to parents; drug epidemics; Hale House hotline; Percy Sutton's help; (2) Oval Office visit and impressions of Ronald Reagan; philosophy of life; Conference on the Innocent Child; philosophy of work.
2.7B11	540	ƀƀ	‡a Permission required to cite, quote, and reproduce; contact repository for information.
3.1A2	700	1ƀ	‡a Hale, Clara, ‡d d. 1992, ‡e interviewee.
3.1A2	700	1ƀ	‡a Hale, Lorraine, ‡e interviewee.
3.3C	700	1ƀ	‡a Murray, James Briggs, ‡e interviewer.

Oral history project

Main entry (Chapter 3)

New York City Immigrant Labor Oral History Project.

Description

Oral history interviews of the New York City Immigrant Labor Oral History Project, 1973–1975.

570 sound cassettes (ca. 60 min. each)

The project began in 1973 under a two-year grant from the National Endowment for the Humanities. Interviews were conducted by undergraduate City College students taught by Virginia Yans and Leon Fink, social history students of Yans and Herbert Gutman at CUNY Graduate Center, and graduate student staff interviewers. Interviewers visited nursing homes such as the Workmen's Circle Home and union retiree groups including the ILGWU Cloak Worker's Union and Longshoremen's Local 1814 to search out and tape immigrant workers whose memories dated to the turn of the century. The project focused on contrasting experiences of white ethnic and black newcomers to New York and the community, cultural, and work lives of immigrants. Institutional history was not a priority.

The collection consists of 285 interviews with American Black, Irish, Italian, Jewish, and Scandinavian immigrant workers. Topics include: family life, education, assimilation, work process, women's roles, ethnic community relations, pre-immigration experiences, work in the garment industry and on the docks, living conditions, politics, leisure, religion, unions, Ellis Island, courtship, class.

All tapes are open for research but interviewees may not be cited by name.

Indexes and partial transcripts available.

Professor Herbert Gutman, project director, donated the tapes of the New York City Immigrant Labor Oral History Project in 1983. They were transferred from the New Jersey Historical Commission where they had been temporarily housed.

Added entries (Chapter 3)

Gutman, Herbert George, 1928–

Oral history project—USMARC tagging

Rule no.	Tag	Ind.	Field contents
3.1B	110	2b	‡a New York City Immigrant Labor Oral History Project.
2.1B1–2.1B4	245	00	‡a Oral history interviews of the New York City Immigrant Labor Oral History Project, ‡f 1973-1975.
2.5C1–2.1C2	300	bb	‡a 570 sound cassettes (ca. 60 min. each)
2.7B1, 2.7B2, 2.7B3	520	bb	‡a The project began in 1973 under a two-year grant from the National Endowment for the Humanities. Interviews were conducted by undergraduate City College students taught by Virginia Yans and Leon Fink, social history students of Yans and Herbert Gutman at CUNY Graduate Center, and graduate student staff interviewers. Interviewers visited nursing homes such as the Workmen's Circle Home and union retiree groups including the ILGWU Cloak Worker's Union and Longshoremen's Local 1814 to search out and tape immigrant workers whose memories dated to the turn of the century. The project focused on contrasting experiences of white ethnic and black newcomers to New York and the community, cultural, and work lives of immigrants. Institutional history was not a priority.
2.7B3	520	8b	‡a The collection consists of 285 interviews with American Black, Irish, Italian, Jewish, and Scandinavian immigrant workers. Topics include: family life, education, assimilation, work process, women's roles, ethnic community relations, pre-immigration experiences, work in the garment industry and on the docks, living conditions, politics, leisure, religion, unions, Ellis Island, courtship, class.
2.7B10, 2.7B11	540	bb	‡a All tapes are open for research but interviewees may not be cited by name.
2.7B12	555	0b	‡a Indexes and partial transcripts available.
2.7B8	561	bb	‡a Professor Herbert Gutman, project director, donated the tapes of the New York City Immigrant Labor Oral History Project in 1983. They were transferred from the New Jersey Historical Commission where they had been temporarily housed.
3.2A	700	1b	‡a Gutman, Herbert George, ‡d 1928-

Oral history project

Main entry (Chapter 3)

Role of DARPA/IPTO in the Development of Computer Science Project.

Description (chapters 1 and 2)

Oral history interviews of the Role of DARPA/IPTO in the Development of Computer Science Project, 1989–1991.

Sound recordings: 65 sound cassettes (ca. 60 min. each) : analog, mono.

Transcripts: 46 v.

The Information Processing Techniques Office (IPTO) of the Defense Advanced Research Projects Agency (DARPA) was established in 1962 to engage in information technology research and to develop new computer systems for the Department of Defense. When DARPA was reorganized in 1986, IPTO ceased to be a discrete office. The Charles Babbage Institute of the University of Minnesota was chosen to conduct research and write a history of the office (NASA-Ames Research Grant NAG 2-532, subcontract USC/PO 473764). Arthur L. Norberg, the Institute's director, headed the project, which was assisted by an IPTO History Committee. The resulting document was submitted to DARPA in 1992.

The project conducted 46 interviews with individuals associated with DARPA/IPTO, or with projects supported by the office. The interviews were done between 1989 and 1991 by Arthur L. Norberg, Judy E. O'Neill, Kerry J. Freedman, and William Aspray, all of whom served as researchers on the Role of DARPA/IPTO Project.

Interviewers discuss the activities of DARPA/IPTO in the development of data processing, computer science, artificial intelligence, time-sharing, and networking (including the ARPA network), primarily during the period from 1962 to 1985.

Individual interviews in this collection have been cataloged separately.

Forthcoming book: Arthur L. Norberg and Judy E. O'Neill. Creating Radical Visions of Future Technology: DARPA's Role in Changing Computing.

Added entries (Chapter 3)

Aspray, William, interviewer.
Norberg, Arthur Lawrence, 1938– interviewer.
O'Neill, Judy E. (Judy Elizabeth), interviewer.
Freedman, Kerry, interviewer.
Charles Babbage Institute.

Oral history project—USMARC tagging

Rule no.	*Tag*	*Ind.*	*Field contents*
3.1B	110	2ʰ	ǂa Role of DARPA/IPTO in the Development of Computer Science Project.
2.1B1–2.1B4	245	00	ǂa Oral history interviews of the Role of DARPA/IPTO in the Development of Computer Science Project, ǂf 1989-1991.
2.5C1–2.5C3, 2.5C6, 2.5E	300	ʰʰ	ǂ3 Sound recordings: ǂa 65 sound cassettes (ca. 60 min. each) : ǂb analog, mono.
2.5B1, 2.5E	300	ʰʰ	ǂ3 Transcripts: ǂa 46 v.
2.7B1, 2.7B2	500	ʰʰ	ǂb The Information Processing Techniques Office (IPTO) of the Defense Advanced Research Projects Agency (DARPA) was established in 1962 to engage in information technology research and to develop new computer systems for the Department of Defense. When DARPA was reorganized in 1986, IPTO ceased to be a discrete office. The Charles Babbage Institute of the University of Minnesota was chosen to conduct research and write a history of the office (NASA-Ames Research Grant NAG 2-532, subcontract USC/PO 473764). Arthur L. Norberg, the Institute's director, headed the project, which was assisted by an IPTO History Committee. The resulting document was submitted to DARPA in 1992.
2.7B2	500	ʰʰ	ǂa The project conducted 46 interviews with individuals associated with DARPA/IPTO, or with projects supported by the office. The interviews were done between 1989 and 1991 by Arthur L. Norberg, Judy E. O'Neill, Kerry J. Freedman, and William Aspray, all of whom served as researchers on the Role of DARPA/IPTO Project.
2.7B3	520	8ʰ	ǂa Interviewers discuss the activities of DARPA/IPTO in the development of data processing, computer science, artificial intelligence, time-sharing, and networking (including the ARPA network), primarily during the period from 1962 to 1985.
2.7B16	500	ʰʰ	ǂa Individual interviews in this collection have been cataloged separately.
2.7B15	581	8ʰ	ǂa Forthcoming book: Arthur L. Norberg and Judy E. O'Neill. Creating Radical Visions of Future Technology: DARPA's Role in Changing Computing.
3.3C	700	1ʰ	ǂa Aspray, William, ǂe interviewer.
3.3C	700	1ʰ	ǂa Norberg, Arthur L. ǂq (Arthur Lawrence), ǂd 1938- ǂe interviewer.
3.3C	700	1ʰ	ǂa O'Neill, Judy E. ǂq (Judy Elizabeth), ǂe interviewer.
3.3C	700	1ʰ	ǂa Freedman, Kerry, ǂe interviewer.
3.3D	710	2ʰ	ǂa Charles Babbage Institute.

Oral history project

Main entry (Chapter 3)

Minnesota Farm Advocate Program Oral History Project.

Description (chapters 1 and 2)

Oral history interviews of the Minnesota Farm Advocate Program Oral History Project, 1988–1989.

Sound recordings: 37 sound cassettes (ca. 90 min. each)

Transcripts: 31 v.

Interviewed 1988–1989 by Dianna Hunter for the Minnesota Farm Advocate Program Oral History Project.

Thirty-one interviews with men and women involved with farm advocacy problems and programs in Minnesota. Different personal styles of advocacy become evident as the narrators discuss important topics such as mediation and negotiation. Working with farmers who have diverse ideas and personalities often creates frustrations for the advocates who are trying to promote cooperation between the advocates and different agencies. These frustrations are described along with the emotional rewards that come with helping communities. Trends of farm advocacy and the historical roots of the trends are discussed, and agricultural law is touched upon. Organizations such as the Farmer's Home Administration and the Minnesota Farm Advocate Program are discussed as well as the farm activist group Groundswell.

Individual interviews in this collection have been cataloged separately.

No interviews may be used in screenplays or theatrical or dramatic performances until 15 August 2001. Some interviews may be subject to other restrictions.

Interview description sheets are available in the repository, filed in the oral history notebooks as OH 142.

Publications: Dianna Hunter. Breaking Hard Ground: Stories of Minnesota Farm Advocates.

Added entries (Chapter 3)

Hunter, Dianna, 1949– interviewer.

Minnesota Farm Advocate Program.

Oral history project—USMARC tagging

Rule no.	Tag	Ind.	Field contents
3.1B	110	2♭	‡a Minnesota Farm Advocate Program Oral History Project.
2.1B1–2.1B4	245	00	‡a Oral history interviews of the Minnesota Farm Advocate Program Oral History Project, ‡f 1988–1989.
2.5C1–2.5C2, 2.5E	300	♭♭	‡3 Sound recordings: ‡a 37 sound cassettes (ca. 90 min. each)
2.5B1, 2.5E	300	♭♭	‡3 Transcripts: ‡a 31 v.
2.7B2	500	♭♭	‡a Interviewed 1988–1989 by Dianna Hunter for the Minnesota Farm Advocate Program Oral History Project.
2.7B3	520	♭♭	‡a Thirty-one interviews with men and women involved with farm advocacy problems and programs in Minnesota. ‡b Different personal styles of advocacy become evident as the narrators discuss important topics such as mediation and negotiation. Working with farmers who have diverse ideas and personalities often creates frustrations for the advocates who are trying to promote cooperation between the advocates and different agencies. These frustrations are described along with the emotional rewards that come with helping communities. Trends of farm advocacy and the historical roots of the trends are discussed, and agricultural law is touched upon. Organizations such as the Farmer's Home Administration and the Minnesota Farm Advocate Program are discussed as well as the farm activist group Groundswell.
2.7B16	500	♭♭	‡a Individual interviews in this collection have been cataloged separately.
2.7B11	540	♭♭	‡a No interviews may be used in screenplays or theatrical or dramatic performances until 15 August 2001. Some interviews may be subject to other restrictions.
2.7B12	555	0♭	‡a Interview description sheets are available in the repository, filed in the oral history notebooks as OH 142.
2.7B15	581	♭♭	‡a Dianna Hunter. Breaking Hard Ground: Stories of Minnesota Farm Advocates.
3.3C	700	1♭	‡a Hunter, Dianna, ‡d 1949- ‡e interviewer.
3.3D	710	2♭	‡a Minnesota Farm Advocate Program.

Oral history project

Main entry (Chapter 3)

New York Motion Picture Industry Oral History Project.

Description (chapters 1 and 2)

Oral history interviews of the New York Motion Picture Industry Oral History Project, 1963–1985.

125 sound tape reels.

12 videoreels.

Project sponsored by American Museum of the Moving Image to gather information from people involved with the motion picture industry in New York City, particularly as it relates to Astoria Studios.

Interviews with people involved in professions associated with the motion picture industry in New York City, especially those pertaining to Astoria Studios. Some of the founders of Astoria Motion Picture and Television Foundation are interviewed. Professions include directors, producers, screen writers, cameramen, business agents, electricians, songwriters, casting directors, editors, actors, artists, songwriters, costume designers, projectionists, and propmen. Some of the interviews deal with the Astoria Studios during the time it was the Army Pictorial Center. Others are interviews with people associated with recent pictures such as *Just Tell Me What You Want*, and *Wolfen*. A few interviewees are members of the Union of Motion Picture Craftsmen. Some people were interviewed by staff members of the museum, and many interviews have been transcribed, 1963–1981. Also includes video tapes of interviews with Sylvia Sidney, 1985, and Rouben Mamoulian, 1984.

Unpublished guide.

Added entries (Chapter 3)

American Museum of the Moving Image.

Sidney, Sylvia, interviewee.

Mamoulian, Rouben, interviewee.

Oral history project—USMARC tagging

Rule no.	Tag	Ind.	Field contents
3.1B	110	2ҍ	‡a New York Motion Picture Industry Oral History Project.
2.1B1–2.1B4	245	00	‡a Oral history interviews of the New York Motion Picture Industry Oral History Project, ‡f 1963-1985.
2.5C1, 2.5E	300	ҍҍ	‡a 125 sound tape reels.
2.5D1, 2.5E	300	ҍҍ	‡a 12 videoreels.
2.7B2	500	ҍҍ	‡a Project sponsored by American Museum of the Moving Image to gather information from people involved with the motion picture industry in New York City, particularly as it relates to Astoria Studios.
2.7B3	520	0ҍ	‡a Interviews with people involved in professions associated with the motion picture industry in New York City, especially those pertaining to Astoria Studios. Some of the founders of Astoria Motion Picture and Television Foundation are interviewed. ‡b Professions include directors, producers, screen writers, cameramen, business agents, electricians, songwriters, casting directors, editors, actors, artists, songwriters, costume designers, projectionists, and propmen. Some of the interviews deal with the Astoria Studios during the time it was the Army Pictorial Center. Others are interviews with people associated with recent pictures such as JUST TELL ME WHAT YOU WANT, and WOLFEN. A few interviewees are members of the Union of Motion Picture Craftsmen. Some people were interviewed by staff members of the museum, and many interviews have been transcribed, 1963-1981. Also includes video tapes of interviews with Sylvia Sidney, 1985, and Rouben Mamoulian, 1984.
2.7B12	555	0ҍ	‡a Unpublished guide.
3.3D	710	2ҍ	‡a American Museum of the Moving Image.
3.3B	700	1ҍ	‡a Sidney, Sylvia, ‡e interviewee.
3.3B	700	1ҍ	‡a Mamoulian, Rouben, ‡e interviewee.

Oral history collection

Description (chapters 1 and 2)

General physics topics oral history collection, surnames T–Z, [ca. 1960]–1988.

87 sound tape reels.

Interviews with scientists on a wide variety of topics in physics and allied sciences, conducted by or for the American Institute of Physics. Areas covered extensively include radio astronomy; high energy physics theory, experiments, and accelerators; fusion energy research; optics, acoustics, and geophysics; physics societies and other organizations; physics education; refugees from fascism; the development of nuclear weapons; physics in industry; and science policy since World War II.

Scientists interviewed include Ernst Telschow, Edward Teller, Laszlo Tisza, Charles Hard Townes, Merle Antony Tuve, Albrecht Otto Johannes Unsöld, Harold Clayton Urey, Joseph Valasek, John Hasbrouck Van Vleck, John Verhoogen, George Wood Vinal, Chih Hsing Wang, Wallace Waterfall, Harold Worthington Webb, Clyde Edward Weigand, Victor Frederick Weisskopf, Freiherr von Friedrich Carl Weizsäcker, Milton Grandison White, Eugene Paul Wigner, David Todd Wilkinson, Denys Haigh Wilkinson, Harold Albert Wilson, Robert Rathbun Wilson, and Albert Beaumont Wood.

Most interviews have been transcribed.

Name and subject index.

Added entries (Chapter 3)

American Institute of Physics.

(Also make added entries for any or all of the interviewees listed above.)

Oral history collection—USMARC tagging

Rule no.	Tag	Ind.	Field contents
2.1C1–2.1C4, 3.1C	245	00	‡a General physics topics oral history collection, surnames T-Z, ‡f [ca. 1960]-1988.
2.5C1–2.5C2	300	bb	‡a 87 sound tape reels (ca. 30-60 min. each)
2.7B2, 2.7B3	520	0b	‡a Interviews with scientists on a wide variety of topics in physics and allied sciences, conducted by or for the American Institute of Physics. ‡b Areas covered extensively include radio astronomy; high energy physics theory, experiments, and accelerators; fusion energy research; optics, acoustics, and geophysics; physics societies and other organizations; physics education; refugees from fascism; the development of nuclear weapons; physics in industry; and science policy since World War II.
2.7B3	520	8b	‡a Scientists interviewed include Ernst Telschow, Edward Teller, Laszlo Tisza, Charles Hard Townes, Merle Antony Tuve, Albrecht Otto Johannes Unsöld, Harold Clayton Urey, Joseph Valasek, John Hasbrouck Van Vleck, John Verhoogen, George Wood Vinal, Chih Hsing Wang, Wallace Waterfall, Harold Worthington Webb, Clyde Edward Weigand, Victor Frederick Weisskopf, Freiherr von Friedrich Carl Weizsäcker, Milton Grandison White, Eugene Paul Wigner, David Todd Wilkinson, Denys Haigh Wilkinson, Harold Albert Wilson, Robert Rathbun Wilson, and Albert Beaumont Wood.
2.7B16	500	bb	‡a Most interviews have been transcribed.
2.7B12	555	0b	‡a Name and subject index.
3.3D	710	2b	‡a American Institute of Physics.

(Also make added entries for any or all of the interviewees listed above.)

Oral history collection

Description (chapters 1 and 2)

Woodstock artists oral history collection, 1962–1975.

22 sound cassettes (ca. 60 min. each)

Taped interviews with thirty-seven Woodstock artists, originally done by Karl Fortess for the School of Fine and Applied Arts at Boston University, 1966–1975, and covering the topics of background and training, identification with society, work patterns, interests, teachers and/or influences, attitudes toward teaching, and opinions of contemporary trends. Artists include Arnold and Lucile Blanc, Alexander Brook, Adolf Dehn, Philip Guston, Doris Lee, Henry Mattson, William Pachner, Bernard Steffen, and Dorothy Varian. Interview with Alf Evers on the founding of the art colony at Woodstock, including the Byrdcliffe and Maverick colonies, 1972. Interview of Konrad and Florence Cramer by Sam Eskin concerning their lives in relation to Woodstock, 1962.

Name list for Fortess tapes.

Added entries (Chapter 3)

Fortess, Karl, interviewer.

Boston University. School of Fine and Applied Arts.

Oral history collection—USMARC tagging

Rule no.	Tag	Ind.	Field contents
2.1C1–2.1C4, 3.1C	245	00	‡a Woodstock artists oral history collection, ‡f 1962-1975.
	300	ƀƀ	‡a 22 sound cassettes (ca. 60 min. each)
2.7B2, 2.7B3	520	0ƀ	‡a Taped interviews with thirty-seven Woodstock artists, originally done by Karl Fortess for the School of Fine and Applied Arts at Boston University, 1966-1975, and covering the topics of background and training, identification with society, work patterns, interests, teachers and/or influences, attitudes toward teaching, and opinions of contemporary trends. Artists include Arnold and Lucile Blanc, Alexander Brook, Adolf Dehn, Philip Guston, Doris Lee, Henry Mattson, William Pachner, Bernard Steffen, and Dorothy Varian. Interview with Alf Evers on the founding of the art colony at Woodstock, including the Byrdcliffe and Maverick colonies, 1972. Interview of Konrad and Florence Cramer by Sam Eskin concerning their lives in relation to Woodstock, 1962.
2.7B12	555	0ƀ	‡a Name list for Fortess tapes.
3.3C	700	1ƀ	‡a Fortess, Karl, ‡e interviewer.
3.3D	710	2ƀ	‡a Boston University. ‡b School of Fine and Applied Arts.

Oral history collection

Description (chapters 1 and 2)

Hispanic apparel union officers oral history collection, 1983–1984.
23 sound cassettes (60-90 min. each)

The interviews were conducted by Geoffrey Fox as part of a study entitled "Hispanic Organizers and Business Agents," published as an occasional paper of New York University's Center for Latin American and Caribbean Studies in 1984. The study explores how Hispanic immigrants are assimilated into labor organizations and how they, in the process, adapt and reform these organizations for themselves.

The collection consists of interviews in English and Spanish with 26 organizers, most of whom work for the Amalgamated Clothing and Textile Workers Union and the International Ladies' Garment Workers Union. Except for four New York-born Puerto Ricans, all interviewees are immigrants from Latin America: Puerto Rico, the Dominican Republic, Costa Rica, Ecuador, Chile, and Honduras. They discuss their careers, experiences in the industry and unions, organizing methods, and views of the labor movement.

Some of the interviews are restricted.

Partial transcriptions available, shelf list available.

Donated by Geoffrey Fox in 1984.

Added entries (Chapter 3)

Fox, Geoffrey, interviewer.

Oral history collection—USMARC tagging

Rule no.	Tag	Ind.	Field contents
2.1C1–2.1C4, 3.1C	245	00	‡a Hispanic apparel union officers oral history collection, ‡f 1983-1984.
2.5C1–2.5C2	300	ƀƀ	‡a 23 sound cassettes (60-90 min. each)
2.7B2, 2.7B3, 2.7B15	520	ƀƀ	‡a The interviews were conducted by Geoffrey Fox as part of a study entitled "Hispanic Organizers and Business Agents," published as an occasional paper of New York University's Center for Latin American and Caribbean Studies in 1984. The study explores how Hispanic immigrants are assimilated into labor organizations and how they, in the process, adapt and reform these organizations for themselves.
2.7B1, 2.7B3	520	0ƀ	‡a The collection consists of interviews in English and Spanish with 26 organizers, most of whom work for the Amalgamated Clothing and Textile Workers Union and the International Ladies' Garment Workers Union. Except for four New York-born Puerto Ricans, all interviewees are immigrants from Latin America: Puerto Rico, the Dominican Republic, Costa Rica, Ecuador, Chile, and Honduras. They discuss their careers, experiences in the industry and unions, organizing methods, and views of the labor movement.
2.7B10	506	ƀƀ	‡a Some of the interviews are restricted.
2.7B12	555	0ƀ	‡a Partial transcriptions available, shelf list available.
2.7B9	541	ƀƀ	‡a Donated by Geoffrey Fox in 1984.
3.3C	700	1ƀ	‡a Fox, Geoffrey E., ‡e interviewer.

Oral history collection

Description (chapters 1 and 2)

Black aviators oral history collection, 1989–1990.

4 videocassettes (7 hr.)

2 items (200 p.)

Throughout the 1930s black Americans struggled to gain the opportunity and right to fly airplanes. Despite widespread racism and sexism during that decade, their efforts resulted in a tenfold increase in the number of licensed black pilots, and led the federal government to sanction black male participation in aviation during World War II.

During 1989 and 1990, Theodore Robinson, National Air and Space Museum, conducted videotaped interviews with five black aviators on their experiences in the 1930s. C. Alfred Anderson, Janet Harmon Bragg, Cornelius Coffey, Harold Hurd, and Lewis A. Jackson explain how they obtained airplanes and training, publicized their aviation skills, and contended with social and institutional prejudices. Visual documentation includes group interaction and photographs.

Name index to transcript.

Added entries (Chapter 3)

Anderson, C. Alfred, interviewee.

Bragg, Janet Harmon, interviewee.

Coffey, Cornelius, interviewee.

Hurd, Harold, interviewee.

Jackson, Lewis A., interviewee.

Robinson, Theodore, interviewer.

Oral history collection—USMARC tagging

Rule no.	*Tag*	*Ind.*	*Field contents*
2.1C1–2.1C4	245	0	ǂa Black aviators oral history collection, ǂf 1989-1990.
2.5D1–2.5D2	300	bb	ǂa 4 videocassettes (7 hr.)
2.5B2	300	bb	ǂa 2 items (200 p.)
2.7B16	500	bb	ǂa Throughout the 1930s black Americans struggled to gain the opportunity and right to fly airplanes. Despite widespread racism and sexism during that decade, their efforts resulted in a tenfold increase in the number of licensed black pilots, and led the federal government to sanction black male participation in aviation during World War II.
2.7B1, 2.7B2, 2.7B3	520	0b	ǂb During 1989 and 1990, Theodore Robinson, National Air and Space Museum, conducted videotaped interviews with five black aviators on their experiences in the 1930s. C. Alfred Anderson, Janet Harmon Bragg, Cornelius Coffey, Harold Hurd, and Lewis A. Jackson explain how they obtained airplanes and training, publicized their aviation skills, and contended with social and institutional prejudices. Visual documentation includes group interaction and photographs.
2.7B12	555	0b	ǂa Name index to transcript.
3.3B	700	1b	ǂa Anderson, C. Alfred, ǂe interviewee.
3.3B	700	1b	ǂa Bragg, Janet Harmon, ǂe interviewee.
3.3B	700	1b	ǂa Coffey, Cornelius, ǂe interviewee.
3.3B	700	1b	ǂa Hurd, Harold, ǂe interviewee.
3.3B	700	1b	ǂa Jackson, Lewis A., ǂe interviewee.
3.3C	700	1b	ǂa Robinson, Theodore, ǂe interviewer.

Repository's entire holdings

Main entry (Chapter 3)

Greenup County Public Library. South Shore Branch.

Description (chapters 1 and 2)

Oral history collection of the Greenup County Public Library, South Shore Branch (Kentucky), 1976–1981.

18 sound cassettes (16 hr.)

Interviews were conducted by Library staff members and others participating in the Kentucky Oral History Commission's taping programs, developed during the American Revolution Bicentennial to promote interest in state and local history.

These interviews of South Shore and northern Greenup County residents relate to the general history and development of the area.

Subjects include South Shore merchants and businesspersons, local political figures, and representatives of other occupations and professions. Interviews generally focus on the historic development of South Shore, Greenup County, and the Big Sandy River region. Interviewees include John P. Davis, Paul Hannah, Gertrude Hill, Orville Howerton, Nellie McMullen, and Avis Van Bibber.

Item list.

Added entries (Chapter 3)

Davis, John P., interviewee.
Hannah, Paul, interviewee.
Hill, Gertrude, interviewee.
Howerton, Orville, interviewee.
McMullen, Nellie, interviewee.
Van Bibber, Avis, interviewee.

Repository's entire holdings—USMARC tagging

Rule no.	*Tag*	*Ind.*	*Field contents*
3.1D	110	2ᵇ	‡a Greenup County Public Library. ‡b South Shore Branch.
2.1D1–2.1D4	245	00	‡a Oral history collection of the Greenup County Public Library, South Shore Branch (Kentucky), ‡f 1976–1981.
2.5C1–2.5C2	300	ᵇᵇ	‡a 18 sound cassettes (16 hr.)
2.7B2	500	ᵇᵇ	‡a Interviews were conducted by Library staff members and others participating in the Kentucky Oral History Commission's taping programs, developed during the American Revolution Bicentennial to promote interest in state and local history.
2.7B3	520	ᵇᵇ	‡a These interviews of South Shore and northern Greenup County residents relate to the general history and development of the area.
2.7B3	520	8ᵇ	‡a Subjects include South Shore merchants and businesspersons, local political figures, and representatives of other occupations and professions. Interviews generally focus on the historic development of South Shore, Greenup County, and the Big Sandy River region. Interviewees include John P. Davis, Paul Hannah, Gertrude Hill, Orville Howerton, Nellie McMullen, and Avis Van Bibber.
2.7B12	555	0ᵇ	‡a Item list.
3.3B	700	1ᵇ	‡a Davis, John P., ‡e interviewee.
3.3B	700	1ᵇ	‡a Hannah, Paul, ‡e interviewee.
3.3B	700	1ᵇ	‡a Hill, Gertrude, ‡e interviewee.
3.3B	700	1ᵇ	‡a Howerton, Orville, ‡e interviewee.
3.3B	700	1ᵇ	‡a McMullen, Nellie, ‡e interviewee.
3.3B	700	1ᵇ	‡a Van Bibber, Avis, ‡e interviewee.

Repository's entire holdings

Main entry (Chapter 3)

Herbert H. Lehman College. Bronx Institute. Archives.

Description (chapters 1 and 2)

Oral history collection of the Bronx Institute Archives of Lehman College Library, CUNY (City University of New York), 1981–1991.

Sound recordings: 45 sound cassettes (ca. 69-90 min. each)

Transcripts: 165 v.

Tapes and transcripts (ca. 40% transcribed) of some 410 oral history interviews conducted by the institute with residents of Bronx neighborhoods such as Williamsbridge, South Bronx, Fordham, Belmont, Clason Point, Tremont, Riverdale, Morrisania, and others. Topics typically discussed in the interviews include education, employment, ethnic relations, family life and customs, health care, housing, landmarks, leisure activities, mass transportation, private and public institutions, and the periods covering World War I and II. Interviewees were drawn from knowledgeable and long time Bronx residents; community activists; and civic, business, political and institution leaders. The Bronx Institute was formerly known as the Bronx Regional and Community History Institute.

Personal papers (e.g., letters, photographs, deeds, programs, bills) and organizational archives (Amalgamated Housing Corporation, Riverdale Neighborhood House) often supplement and provide further documentation of the oral histories.

Some tapes are restricted.

Tapes and transcripts may not be duplicated.

Indexed by name, neighborhood, and subjects discussed.

Added entries (Chapter 3)

Bronx Regional and Community History Institute.

Repository's entire holdings - USMARC tagging

Rule no.	Tag	Ind.	Field contents
3.1D	110	2♭	‡a Herbert H. Lehman College. ‡b Bronx Institute. ‡b Archives.
2.1D1–2.1D4	245	00	‡a Oral history collection of the Bronx Institute Archives of Lehman College Library, CUNY (City University of New York), ‡a 1981-1991.
2.5C1–2.5C2, 2.5E	300	♭♭	‡3 Sound recordings: ‡a 45 sound cassettes (ca. 69-90 min. each)
2.5B2	300	♭♭	‡3 Transcripts: ‡a 165 v.
2.7B1, 2.7B2, 2.7B3	520	♭♭	‡a Tapes and transcripts (ca. 40% transcribed) of some 410 oral history interviews conducted by the institute with residents of Bronx neighborhoods such as Williamsbridge, South Bronx, Fordham, Belmont, Clason Point, Tremont, Riverdale, Morrisania, and others. ‡b Topics typically discussed in the interviews include education, employment, ethnic relations, family life and customs, health care, housing, landmarks, leisure activities, mass transportation, private and public institutions, and the periods covering World War I and II. Interviewees were drawn from knowledgeable and long time Bronx residents; community activists; and civic, business, political and institution leaders. The Bronx Institute was formerly known as the Bronx Regional and Community History Institute.
2.7B16	500	♭♭	‡a Personal papers (e.g., letters, photographs, deeds, programs, bills) and organizational archives (Amalgamated Housing Corporation, Riverdale Neighborhood House) often supplement and provide further documentation of the oral histories.
2.7B10	506	♭♭	‡a Some tapes are restricted.
2.7B11	540	♭♭	‡a Tapes and transcripts may not be duplicated.
2.7B12	555	♭♭	‡a Indexed by name, neighborhood, and subjects discussed.
3.3D	710	2♭	‡a Bronx Regional and Community History Institute.

Table of USMARC Equivalents for Descriptive Elements

Table 1 – Descriptive element and rule to USMARC field

The elements below are given in the order in which they appear in the cataloging manual.

Descriptive element	Field/subfield
Title (2.1)	245
Form element (2.1A2, 2.1B2, 2.1C2, 2.1D2)	245 ǂa
Name element (2.1A3, 2.1B3, 2.1C3, 2.1D3)	245 ǂa
Date element (2.1A4, 2.1B4, 2.1C4, 2.1D4)	245 ǂf
General material designation (2.1E)	245 ǂh
Physical description (2.5)	
Transcripts	
Single volume or item (transcripts) (2.5B1)	300 ǂa
Multiple volumes or items (transcripts) (2.5B2)	300 ǂa
Dimensions (transcripts) (2.5B3)	300 ǂc
Electronic form (transcripts) (2.5B4)	300 ǂa, ǂc
Sound recordings (2.5C)	
Type of sound recording medium and number of physical units (2.5C1)	300 ǂa
Playing time (2.5C2)	300 ǂa
Type of recording (e.g., analog, digital) (2.5C3)	300 ǂb
Playing speed (2.5C4)	300 ǂb
Number of tracks (2.5C5)	300 ǂb
Number of sound channels (2.5C6)	300 ǂb
Dimensions (2.5C7)	300 ǂc
Videorecordings (2.5D)	
Type of recording medium and number of physical units (2.5D1)	300 ǂa
Playing time (2.5D2)	300 ǂa
Color (2.5D3)	300 ǂb
Dimensions (2.5D4)	300 ǂc
Multiple formats, introductory wording for form of material (2.5E)	300 ǂ3

Descriptive element	Field/subfield
Supplementary material (2.5F)	500 or 520
Notes (2.7)	
Biographical information (2.7B1)	545
Interview details (2.7B2)	500
Scope and content/Abstract (2.7B3)	520
Linking entry complexity (2.7B4)	580
Additional physical form available (2.7B5)	530
Reproduction (2.7B6)	533
Location of originals/duplicates (2.7B7)	535
Provenance (2.7B8)	561
Immediate source of acquisition (2.7B9)	541
Restrictions on access (2.7B10)	506
Terms governing use and reproduction (2.7B11)	540
Cumulative index/finding aids (2.7B12)	555
Citation (2.7B13)	510
Preferred citation of described materials (2.7B14)	524
Publications (2.7B15)	581
General note (2.7B16)	500
Combined notes (2.7B)	500 or 520
Main entries	
Interviewees, collectors (personal names, 3.1A, 3.1C)	100
Relator terms (*interviewee, collector*)	700 ‡e
Project names (3.1B)	110
Repository names (3.1D)	110
Added entries	
Interviewees, personal names (3.3A, 3.3B)	700
Interviewers, personal names (3.3C)	700
Relator term (*interviewer*)	700 ‡e
Corporate bodies associated with an oral history project or collection (3.3D)	710
Project names (corporate names, 3.3E)	710
Alternate titles (3.3F)	246
Titles of songs, poems, etc. (title or name-title entries, 3.3F1)	740, 700 , 710

Table 2 – USMARC field to descriptive element and rule

In this table, USMARC fields and subfields are given below in numerical order with citations to equivalent descriptive elements given in the right hand column.

Field/subfield	Descriptive element	Rule
100	Interviewee or collector (personal name main entry)	3.1A, 3.1C
110	Project name (corporate body main entry)	3.1B
110	Repository name (corporate body main entry)	3.1D
245	Title	2.1
‡a	Name element	2.1A2, 2.1B2, 2.1C2, 2.1D2
‡a	Form element	2.1A3, 2.1B3, 2.1C3, 2.1D3
‡f	Date element	2.1A4, 2.1B4, 2.1C4, 2.1D4
246	Alternate titles	3.3F
300	Physical description	2.5
‡a	Extent	2.5B1–2, 2.5C1–2, 2.5D1–2
‡b	Other physical details	2.5C3–6, 2.5D3
‡c	Dimensions	2.5B3, 2.5C7, 2.5D4
500	General note	2.7B16
500	Interview details	2.7B2
506	Restrictions on access	2.7B10
510	Citation	2.7B13
520	Scope and content/Abstract	2.7B3
524	Preferred citation	2.7B14
530	Additional physical form available	2.7B4
533	Reproduction	2.7B5
535	Location of originals/duplicates	2.7B6
540	Terms governing use and reproduction	2.7B11
541	Immediate source of acquisition	2.7B9
545	Biographical information	2.7B1
555	Cumulative index/finding aids	2.7B12

Field/subfield	Descriptive element	Rule
561	Provenance	2.7B8
580	Linking entry complexity	2.7B4
581	Publications	2.7B15
700	Interviewees, interviewers (personal name added entry)	3.3A-3.3C
710	Project names, corporate bodies associated (corporate body added entries)	3.3D-3.3E
740, 700, 710	Titles of songs, poems, etc. (title or name-title added entries)	3.3F1

Bibliography

Anglo-American Cataloguing Rules, 2nd ed., 1988 rev. Chicago: American Library Association, 1988.

This is the standard for cataloging materials in general libraries in most English-speaking countries. It covers materials in many physical formats and includes rules for constructing name headings (personal names, corporate names, geographic names).

Archives, Personal Papers, and Manuscripts: A Cataloging Manual for Archival Repositories, Historical Societies, and Manuscript Libraries. 2nd ed. Steven L. Hensen, comp. Chicago: Society of American Archivists, 1990.

This manual is endorsed by the Society of American Archivists as the standard for archival cataloging. It is designed to replace Chapter 4 of *AACR 2* for the cataloging of archival materials using archival control. Also includes rules for constructing name headings (personal names, corporate names, geographic names); these are primarily verbatim selections from *AACR 2*.

Cataloging Unpublished Nonprint Materials: A Manual of Suggestions, Comments, and Examples. By Verna Urbanski, with Bao Chu Chang and Bernard L. Karon. Lake Crystal, Minn.: Soldier Creek Press, 1992.

This manual is intended to be used in conjunction with *AACR 2* for bibliographically-oriented cataloging. Some of the examples in the chapter on sound recordings are for oral history interviews.

Oral History Evaluation Guidelines. Los Angeles: Oral History Association, 1990.

These guidelines provide for the evaluation of oral history programs. Part of the evaluation concerns how well the program meets guidelines relating to description and cataloging.

USMARC Format for Bibliographic Data: Including Guidelines for Content Designation. Washington, D.C.: Library of Congress, 1994.

The complete documentation of the USMARC format for all kinds of materials: books, archival and manuscripts control, computer files, maps, music, visual materials, and serials.

Index

A

Abbreviations, 2.5B2
Abstract (scope and content note), 2.7B3
Abstracts, published, 2.7B13
Access points
  (*see also* Main entries; Added entries)
  choice, Chapter 3
  definition, p. 10, 3.0A
  sources for determining, 3.0B
Access restrictions, 2.7B10
Accession numbers, 2.7B9
Acquisition, source of, 2.7B9
Added entries
  definition, 3.0A
  general rules, 3.2
  interviewees, 3.3A
  interviewers, 3.3C
  justified in description, 3.0B, 3.2C
  projects, 3.3E
Additional physical form available note, 2.7B5
Alternate title, *see* Title
Anglo-American Cataloguing Rules (AACR 2), p. 3,
    p. 4, p. 12, p. 13
  use for name headings, 3.0A, 3.2B
  use for physical description, 2.5A3, 2.5C1, 2.5D1
  when to use, p. 6
Archives, Personal Papers, and Manuscripts (APPM),
    p. 3, p. 4, p. 12, p. 13
  use for name headings, 3.0A, 3.2B
  when to use, p. 6, 2.6
Areas of description, definition, p. 4
Availability of copies, notes concerning, 2.7B5

B

Bibliographic citations, in notes, 2.7B13
Biographical information, 2.7B1
Brackets, *see* Square brackets

C

Ca., see *Circa*
Capitalization, 2.1
Catalog, definition, p. 9
Catalog record, definition, p. 9
Cataloging
  archival approach, p. 1
  definition, p. 9

Chief source of information, not used, p. 12, 2.0B
Choice of access points, Chapter 3
Circa, use of abbreviation *ca.*
  with approximate playing times, 2.5C2, 2.5D2
  with dates in titles, 2.1A4
Citations, preferred by repository, 2.7B14
  (*see also* Bibliographic citations)
Collections of oral history materials
  corporate bodies associated, 3.3D
  definition, p. 7, 1.1
  entry under name of collector, 3.1C
  entry under title, 3.1C
  titles, 2.1C
  uncertain origin, 3.1E
Collective description
  characteristic of archival cataloging, p. 1, p. 12
  of projects and collections, 1.2
Collector
  as name element in title, 2.1C3
  as relator term, 3.1C
  entry under (main entry), 3.1C
Colons
  following introductory wording, 1.5, 2.5E, 2.7A1
  in notes, 2.7A1
  in physical description, 2.5A1, 2.5C3, 2.5E
Color, in videorecordings, 2.5D3
Commas, *see* Punctuation of description
Component parts (of collections, projects, etc.), 1.2
  added entries for names of projects, 3.3E
  linking hierarchical relationships, 2.7B4
Computer files
  extent, statement of, 2.5B4
  general material designation, 2.1E
Container lists, *see* Finding aids
Containers, physical description, 2.5B2
Content of interviews, notes concerning, 2.7B3
Copies
  description of use copies, 2.5A4
  extent, 2.5A4
  for preservation, notes concerning, 2.7B16
  generations, 2.5A4, 2.5D1
  location of, 2.7B7
Copyright restrictions, 2.7B11
Correspondence, as supplementary material, 2.5F
Cubic footage, *see* Extent, statement of
Cumulative index/finding aids note, 2.7B12
Custody of materials, history of, *see* Provenance

D

Dashes, *see* Punctuation of description
Date(s)
    in notes, 2.7B2
    in titles, 2.1A4, 2.1B4, 2.1C4, 2.1D4
    of acquisition of materials, 2.7B9
    of interviews, projects, etc., 2.7B2
    probable or uncertain, 2.1A4
Date area of description, 2.4
Deposit, as method of acquisition, 2.7B9
Designations, *see* Relator terms
Detail, levels of, in description, 1.3
Dimensions
    punctuation preceding, 2.5A1
    sound recordings, 2.5C7
    transcripts, 2.5B3
    videorecordings, 2.5D4
Donor, notes concerning, 2.7B9
Duplicates, location of, 2.7B7

E

Edition area, not used, p. 4, 2.2
Electronic form, materials in, 2.5B4
Examples
    explanation of, p. 67, 2.7B
    USMARC tagging, p. 67
Extent, statement of, 2.5A2
    cubic or linear feet (transcripts), 2.5B2
    electronic form (transcripts), 2.5B4
    multiple volumes (transcripts), 2.5B2
    originals, 2.5A4
    single and multiple formats, 2.5A3, 2.5E
    single volumes or items (transcripts), 2.5B1

F

Finding aids
    as sources of information for description, 2.0B
    notes concerning, 2.7B12
Form of material, *see* Title, form element
Formats, additional, 2.7B5
Fundamental information
    definition, p. 5
    rules, 1.3A

G

General material designation, 2.1E
General note, 2.7B16
Gifts, as method of acquisition, 2.7B9
Guides, published, 2.7B13
    (*see also* Finding aids)

H

Headings
    definition, p. 10
    form of, 3.0A, 3.2B
Height, *see* Dimensions
Hierarchical relationships between catalog records,
    2.7B4
History of custody, *see* Provenance
Hyphen, *see* Punctuation of description

I

Immediate source of acquisition note, 2.7B9
Inclusive dates, *see* Date(s)
Indexes
    (*see also* Finding aids)
    notes concerning, 2.7B12
    published, references to, 2.7B13
International Standard Bibliographic Description
    (ISBD) punctuation, 1.5
Interview details note, 2.7B2
Interviewees
    added entries, 3.3A, 3.3B
    biographical information, 2.7B1
    designation in headings (relataor terms), 3.3A, 3.3B
    entry under (main entry), 3.1A1
    multiple interviewees, 2.1A3, 2.7B3, 3.1A2, 3.3A,
        3.3B
    name unknown, 2.1A3, 3.1A1
Interviewers
    added entries, 3.1A1, 3.3C
    characterization, 2.7B2
    designation in headings (relator terms), 3.3C
    name(s) given in notes, 2.7B2
Interviews
    date, place, and other details, 2.7B2
    definition, p. 7
Introductory wording
    in notes, 2.7A1, 2.7B4, 2.7B5, 2.7B7, 2.7B13,
        2.7B14, 2.7B15
    in statement of extent, 2.5E
Inventories, *see* Finding aids
ISBD (International Standard Bibliographic
    Description) punctuation, 1.5

L

Language
    of description, 1.4
    of interviews, 2.7B2
Letters (manuscripts), as supplementary material, 2.5F
Levels of description, linking, 2.7B4
Levels of detail in description, 1.3

Library of Congress rule interpretations, p. 13
Linear footage, *see* Extent, statement of
Linking entry complexity notes, 2.7B4
Literary rights restrictions, notes concerning, 2.7B11
Location, in repository holdings titles, 2.1D3

M

Main entries, 3.1
  definition, 3.0A
Material specific details area, not used, p. 4, 2.3
Measurement of extent, *see* Extent, statement of
Memoirs, 2.1A2
Microforms
  general material designation, 2.1E
  reproductions, available in addition to originals,
    2.7B5

N

Name elements in titles, 2.1A3, 2.1B3, 2.1C3, 2.1D3
Name-title added entries, 3.3F1
Narrators, *see* Interviewees
Note area, p. 4, 2.7
Notes, 2.7B
  abstract, 2.7B3
  additional physical form available, 2.7B5
  biographical, 2.7B1
  citation, 2.7B13
  finding aids, 2.7B12
  general note, 2.7B16
  immediate source of acquisition, 2.7B9
  interview details, 2.7B2
  linking entry complexity, 2.7B4
  location of originals/duplicates, 2.7B7
  preferred citation of described materials, 2.7B14
  provenance, 2.7B8
  publications, 2.7B15
  punctuation, 2.7A1
  reproduction, 2.7B6
  restrictions, 2.7B10, 2.7B11
  scope and content, 2.7B3
  separate or combined, 2.7B
  terms governing use and reproduction, 2.7B11

O

Occupations of interviewees, given in notes, 2.7B1
Oral history
  as an intellectual form, p. 1
  definition, p. 7
Oral history collection
  as form element in title, 2.1C2, 2.1D2

Oral history collections, *see* Collections of oral history
  materials
Oral History Evaluation Guidelines, p. 11
Oral history interviews
  (*see also* Interviews)
  definition, p. 7, 1.1
  as form element in title, 2.1A2, 2.1B2
Oral history materials, definition, p. 7, 1.1
Oral history program, definition, p. 7
Oral history projects
  added entries for, 3.3E
  component interviews, 2.7B4
  corporate bodies associated, 3.3D
  definition, p. 8, 2.1B, 1.1
  entry under name of project, 3.1B
  titles, 2.1B
Originals
  disposition after copying, 2.7B6
  field recordings, 2.5A4, 2.7B7
  location, 2.7B7
Other physical details, punctuation preceding, 2.5A1,
  2.5C3
Ownership, transfers of, *see* Provenance

P

Parentheses
  associated punctuation, 1.5
  in statements of extent, 2.5B2, 2.5C2, 2.5D1, 2.5D2
  in titles, 2.1D3
Period, *see* Punctuation of description
Photographs, as supplementary material, 2.5F
Physical description
  guidance from other rules, 2.5C1, 2.5D1
  in notes, 2.7B16
Physical description area, p. 4, 2.5
Physical form, additional, 2.7B5
Place of birth of interviewee, notes concerning, 2.7B1
Place of interview, 2.7B2
Place of residence of interviewee, 2.7B1
Places, given in notes, 2.7B1
Preferred citation of described materials note, 2.7B14
Prescribed punctuation, 1.5
Prescribed sources of information, not used, p. 12, 2.0B
Previous owners, notes concerning, 2.7B8
Price, of acquisition, 2.7B9
Projects
  added entries for, 3.3E
  component interviews, 1.2, 2.7B4
  corporate bodies associated, 3.3D
  definition, p. 7, 1.1, 2.1B
  entry under name of project, 3.1B
  titles, 2.1B

Provenance, p. 1, 1.1
  notes on, 2.7B8
Publication, distribution, etc., area
  described using *AACR 2*, p. 6
Publication, distribution, etc., area, not used, p. 4
Publications based on oral history material, references
  to, 2.7B15
Published descriptions of oral history material,
  references to, 2.7B13
Punctuation of description
  general rules, 1.5
  notes, 2.7A1
  physical description, 2.5A1
  titles, 2.1A4
Purchase, as method of acquisition, 2.7B9

Q

Question mark, with uncertain dates, 2.1A4

R

Reference sources, as sources of information for
  description, 2.0B
References (bibliographic citations)
  to publications based on oral history materials,
    2.7B15
  to publications containing descriptions, etc., of oral
    history materials, 2.7B13
Registers, *see* Finding aids
Relator terms
  collector, 3.1C
  interviewee, 3.1A1, 3.3A, 3.3B
  interviewer, 3.3C, 3.3C
Reminiscences, 2.1A2
Repository
  definition, p. 2
  entire holdings of oral history materials, 2.1D, 3.1D
  entry under (main entry), 3.1D
Reproduction restrictions, notes concerning, 2.7B11
Reproductions
  as additional form available, 2.7B5
  details concerning production, 2.7B6
  location of duplicates, 2.7B7
  physical description, 2.7B6
Residence of interviewee, given in notes, 2.7B1
Responsibility, for creation of oral history materials, 3.1
Restrictions on access, notes concerning, 2.7B10
Restrictions on use and reproduction, notes concerning,
  2.7B11

S

Scope and content of described materials, notes
  concerning, 2.7B3
Scope of rules, p. 2
Semicolons
  (*see also* Punctuation of description)
  in notes, 2.7A1
  in physical description, 2.5A1, 2.5C7
  separating subelements, 1.5, 2.7A1
Series (archival), described using *APPM*, p. 6
Series (bibliographic)
  described using *AACR 2*, p. 6, 2.6
  not used, p. 4, 2.6
Sound recordings
  dimensions, 2.5C7
  extent, 2.5C
  general material designation, 2.1E
  number of sound channels, 2.5C6
  number of tracks, 2.5C5
  playing speed, 2.5C4
  playing time, 2.5C2
  specific material designations, 2.5C1
  type of recording (analog, digital), 2.5C3
  type of recording medium, 2.5C1
Source of acquisition, notes concerning, 2.7B9
Sources
  for determining access points, 3.0B
  of information for description, 2.0B
Spacing, with prescribed punctuation, 1.5, 2.1A4,
    2.5A1, 2.5C3, 2.5C4, 2.5C7, 2.5E, 2.7A1
Span dates, *see* Inclusive dates
Specific material designations
  sound recordings, 2.5C1
  videorecordings, 2.5D1
Sponsorship, notes concerning, 2.7B2
Square brackets
  associated punctuation, 1.5
  not used for supplied titles, 2.1
  with conjectural dates, 2.1A4
Statement of extent, *see* Extent, statement of
Statements of responsibility, not used, 2.1F
Subject
  in notes, 2.7B3
  in titles, 2.1C3
Subject analysis and indexing, not covered, p. 2, p. 10
Subunits of collections and projects, *see* Component
    parts
Summary of content, 2.7B3
Supplementary materials, 2.5F
  in notes, 2.7B16

T

Terms governing use and reproduction, notes concerning, 2.7B11
Title
  added entries, 3.3F
  alternate, 3.3F
  area of description, p. 4, 2.1
  collections, 2.1C
  date element, 2.1A4, 2.1B4, 2.1C4, 2.1D4
  entry under, 3.1A1, 3.1A2, 3.1C, 3.1E
  form element, 2.1A2, 2.1B2, 2.1C2, 2.1D2
  in two languages, 3.3F
  interviews with two or more individuals, 2.1A3
  name element, 2.1A3, 2.1B3, 2.1C3, 2.1D3
  order of elements, 2.1A1, 2.1B1, 2.1C1, 2.1D1
  songs, poems, etc., 3.3F1
  when name of interviewee is unknown, 2.1A3
Topics, given in notes, 2.7B3
Transcribing information from specific sources, not required in oral history cataloging, p. 1, 2.0B
Transcripts
  as sources of information for description, 2.0B
  editorial intervention, 2.2
  extent, statement of, 2.5B
  multiple volumes, folders, or containers, statement of extent, 2.5B2
  pages or leaves, statement of extent, 2.5B1
Transfer of custody, notes concerning, 2.7B8

U

Uncertain dates, 2.1A4
Unit of description, definition, 1.1
Use restrictions, notes concerning, 2.7B11
Users of oral history materials, 1.3B
  access point sought by, 3.2A
USMARC bibliographic format, p. 3, p. 67

V

Videorecordings
  color, 2.5D3
  dimensions, 2.5D4
  extent, statement of, 2.5D
  general material designation, 2.1E
  playback system, 2.5D1
  playing time, 2.5D2
  specific material designations, 2.5D1
  type of recording medium, 2.5D1

W

Width, *see* Dimensions